on track ...

Captain
Beefheart

every album, every song

Opher Goodwin

sonicbondpublishing.com

Sonicbond Publishing Limited
www.sonicbondpublishing.co.uk
Email: info@sonicbondpublishing.co.uk

First Published in the United Kingdom 2022
First Published in the United States 2022

British Library Cataloguing in Publication Data:
A Catalogue record for this book is available from the British Library

Typeset in ITC Garamond & ITC Avant Garde
Printed and bound in England

Graphic design and typesetting: Full Moon Media

*There's no competition with our music. It can't be
compared or impaired, or impaled with points or
justifications... It means absolutely nothing,
just like the sun.*
Don Van Vliet.

Acknowlegements
Thanks to Steve Froy for his encouragement,
corrections and immense knowledge.
Check out 'The Radar Station' at www.beefheart.com.
For further information and anything you want to
know about Captain Beefheart, it's there.

Thanks to Chris Perkins for his editing, and to Liz
Goodwin for her editing and (limited!) patience.

Would you like to write for Sonicbond Publishing?
We are mainly a music publisher, but we also occasionally
publish in other genres including film and television. At Sonicbond
Publishing we are always on the look-out for authors, particularly for
our two main series, On Track and Decades.

Mixing fact with in depth analysis, the On Track series examines
the entire recorded work of a particular musical artist or group. All
genres are considered from easy listening and jazz to 60s soul to 90s
pop, via rock and metal.

The Decades series singles out a particular decade in an artist or
group's history and focuses on that decade in more detail than may
be allowed in the On Track series.

While professional writing experience would, of course, be
an advantage, the most important qualification is to have real
enthusiasm and knowledge of your subject. First-time authors are
welcomed, but the ability to write well in English is essential.

Sonicbond Publishing has distribution throughout Europe and
North America, and all our books are also published in E-book form.
Authors will be paid a royalty based on sales of their book.
Further details about our books are available from
www.sonicbondpublishing.com. To contact us, complete the
contact form there or email info@sonicbondpublishing.co.uk

on track ...
Captain Beefheart

Contents

Introduction

Captain Beefheart and his Magic Band are probably the weirdest band that ever existed, and possibly the best. Many people have described a gig they attended as life-changing. Few would've been as life-changing as my first Captain Beefheart gig.

In 1967 I was 18 years old, supposedly studying for A-levels, but actually undergoing a more serious study of girls, music, Kerouac and the burgeoning underground scene. I was working long shifts through Friday nights at a Lyons bakery, where I met another crazy longhair called Mike. Mike was a little older than me and was seriously into underground music: particularly psychedelia and acid rock. He was a student of English Literature at York University and had the longest hair around: a major credential at the time. He never brushed or combed his hair (believing that it caused split ends), but he ran his fingers through to rid his hair of major tangles. Mike enthused about going to UFO and Middle Earth in London to drop acid and dance all night to bands like Pink Floyd. He was into the West Coast acid rock scene and knew about every band in the Los Angeles/San Francisco area before they'd even released an album. We spent many happy hours sitting in his room, where Mike would fascinate me with the debut albums of The Doors, Country Joe and the Fish, Love and Quicksilver Messenger Service. We were in a world of our own.

Apart from John Peel, who played these jewels on his wonderful late-night radio show Perfumed Garden, no one else seemed to have heard of this treasure trove of music. John Peel championed Captain Beefheart and his Magic Band, claiming they were the best band on the planet. He not only played them on his show but ferried Don and the band around to gigs and introduced them onstage. Peel carried a lot of weight in the underground scene, which is probably why Captain Beefheart and his Magic Band were better known and had more of a following here in Britain than their native USA.

I first heard Beefheart's *Safe As Milk* at Mike's on the day of its release. To say I was bowled over is an understatement. I was into both the blues and psychedelia, but this seemed to combine the two in a way that blasted your mind and body into atoms. It shook me, and I was hooked. I'd never heard anything like it. By this time, I was also going to London underground clubs Middle Earth, UFO, The Roundhouse, The Marquee and Les Cousins. For me, it was to see mainly Pink Floyd, Peter Green's Fleetwood Mac, Jimi Hendrix and Roy Harper. When I heard that Captain Beefheart was going to play at Middle Earth, I was ecstatic. There was only one problem: I was in the midst of my A-level exams. I had been offered a provisional place at university, and needed the grades, but music was more important to me, and besides, my biology exam was a week away. Surely I could afford a night off. High on adrenalin, I drove to London on my trusty motorbike, only to discover that the gig had been postponed. Beefheart's bassist Jerry Handley was ill, and they'd been replaced by the Aynsley Dunbar Retaliation. Now, I quite liked Aynsley Dunbar, but he was no substitute for Captain Beefheart, who was rescheduled for the following week as a double bill with John Mayall (another favourite of mine). That made it an absolute must.

The gig was now going to be the night before my A-level biology exam. If I went, I wouldn't be home until 3:00 a.m., and my exam started at 9:00 a.m.. I would have no last-minute revision, and I'd be knackered. Still, needs must. No choice! It was truly one of the best gigs I have ever been to. I can't remember anything about John Mayall that night, but Beefheart just blew me away! Needless to say, I didn't get the required grade, and the course of my life changed. However, I'd seen Captain Beefheart in all his glory! I wouldn't change that even if I could.

The 1960s were a time of liberal views and creativity. Following World War II and the 1950s austerity, a generation of rebellious teenagers emerged. Fired with optimism, confidence and naivety, they sought to throw off the shackles of conformity and break out from the conservatism of their parents' generation. This was the new age, and young people saw a world of new possibilities, with waves of creativity in fashion, art, writing, dance, architecture and, most of all, music. Social norms were being rejected. There were protests against the Vietnam war, marches for civil rights, a burgeoning spirit of environmentalism, feminism and equality, coupled with a rejection of the establishment. These sparked great social and political change. Young people had a voice, and they wanted to be heard. Minds were opened. Clothes were colourful. Hair was long. Music was loud. The hair, clothes, attitudes and protest weren't a fashion; they were symbols of a new way of living; an alternative to the establishment.

The underground movement had an impact on the mainstream. Young people were dropping out, departing on adventures to exotic third-world countries and delving into new religions and cultures. They were appreciating the world's beauty without needing lots of money. At that time of great social change, many young people were convinced there was a better way to live. They were experimenting with communal living, getting back to nature, dropping out of the rat race, opposing the whole money-driven greed and warmongering attitudes. These were attempts at a simpler, better way of life.

This was the underground culture from which Captain Beefheart and his Magic Band appeared. They were part of the Los Angeles scene, playing at venues like the Avalon Ballroom that catered for the freaks of the day. The West Coast acid rock scene was based around San Francisco and Los Angeles. The two cities had completely opposite vibes, and intense rivalry. San Francisco had more country, jug band, folk roots with bands like Jefferson Airplane, Country Joe and the Fish, Quicksilver Messenger Service and Grateful Dead. Los Angeles had a punkier blues experimental feel, with bands like The Doors, Love, and also Frank Zappa and the Mothers of Invention and Captain Beefheart and his Magic Band, who were more avant-garde.

The counterculture was about being far out. Bands were vying with each other to be more extreme, extolling the underground scene's acid/drug culture. The more outrageous the costumes and hair, the better. A look at the cover of Country Joe and the Fish's *I-Feel-Like-I'm-Fixin'-To-Die* clearly demonstrates that. Captain Beefheart and his Magic Band topped them all. It didn't get any weirder.

So where did this begin? Don Vliet was born on 15 January 1941 in Glendale, California. But in his early teens, the family moved out to the small town of Lancaster, way out in the Mojave Desert. As a boy, he'd always been precocious, heavily immersed in art and sculpture, to the point when at the age of 13, he was offered an all-expenses-paid scholarship to a European college. Don's father had a low opinion of art and artists and turned it down. This didn't deter Don from being involved in art projects in his usual obsessive manner. Once while working on a sculpture, he refused to come out of his room, and demanded that food and drink be passed in to him. Don had a strange relationship with his parents, calling them by their first names, and ordering his mother around as if she was his maid.

Don developed a great liking for blues music, which was unusual for a white kid, particularly in a small desert town like Lancaster. He listened avidly to R&B radio stations and DJ Wolfman Jack's radio station, which pumped out the blues greats like Howlin' Wolf, Jimmy Reed and John Lee Hooker. Don's deep voice and great vocal range were perfect for a similar blues delivery.

At school, he met up with Frank Zappa, who also had an interest in blues, R&B and doo-wop. They began collaborating. Frank was similarly eccentric, experimental, rebellious and go-getting. Nothing was impossible; imagination was the only limitation. The two of them became involved, listening to R&B and doo-wop, playing instruments and singing. In 1963, Don left the restrictions of small-town Lancaster to team up with Frank in Cucamonga, where he'd set up a simple studio. The two of them began working on a number of ambitious projects. There was a doo-wop opera titled 'I Was A Teenage Maltshop' and a film called 'Captain Beefheart vs. The Grunt People' (Grunt People being their name for straight people). Some fragments of these pieces still exist and have been released on a number of albums.

Don adopted the persona Captain Beefheart. He explained that the name came from one of his uncles, who used to lewdly expose himself to Don's girlfriend, saying, 'Aah, what a beauty. It looks just like a fine beef heart'.

The early collaboration with Frank came to an untimely end when his Cucamonga studio was raided by police and Frank arrested for producing pornographic material. He'd been offered $100 to make a sex tape – a sum he couldn't refuse – so he made a sex tape of fake moans from a female friend. He handed over the tape, complete with grunts, squeals and squeaking bedsprings, and was immediately arrested. It was a sting. He had to plead guilty, went to jail for a week, and the police used this as an excuse to ransack his studio. That signalled the end of Frank and Don's ambitious projects, and Don went back to Lancaster.

A number of young kids were getting into the blues, and just like in England, these musicians tended to find each other and form bands. All the members of the *Trout Mask Replica*-era Magic Band had previously played together in Lancaster in a band called Blues in a Bottle. In 1965 – a short while after Don's return from Frank's – local R&B guitar player Alex Snouffer approached Don with the intention of putting together an R&B band. I'm sure Alex didn't know what he was letting himself in for. Don added the Van to his name – thinking it sounded cool – and the first Captain Beefheart and his Magic Band lineup was spawned. As Captain Beefheart was the 'magic man' in those early Frank Zappa collaborations, it was only natural that he should have ownership of the magic band. This was also the start of Don giving the band members their alternative names. For some reason, Alex Snouffer became Alex St. Clair. Could that have had something to do with musician Taj Mahal's real name being Henry St. Claire Fredericks? Was it a mysterious coincidence? Or was it so Alex could have a name that sounded more English? The British Invasion was certainly having an impact.

That first band comprised Don on vocals and blues harp, Alex St. Clair on guitar, Doug Moon on second guitar, Jerry Handley (really an American but reported as being English: probably as a publicity stunt) on bass and Vic Mortensen on drums. Vic was soon replaced by Paul Blakely, and the band immediately began to make an impact in their area. Their English R&B sound captured the zeitgeist of the moment. Their big break came when they played an unlikely gig at the Fourth Annual Teen Fair in spring 1965 and were spotted by a talent scout from the mainstream label A&M: a peculiar label for an increasingly weird-looking underground blues/R&B band. That Teen Fair was the place where Don spied the young Ry Cooder playing with The Rising Sons. Ry was destined to provide the missing thread for the Captain Beefheart sound.

The journey had begun.

The Official Albums
The Legendary A&M Sessions (EP) (1984)

Personnel:
Don Van Vliet: vocals, harmonica
Alex St. Clair Snouffer: drums
Jerry Handley: bass
Doug Moon, Rich Hepner, Alex St. Clair ('Moonchild'): guitar
Paul Blakely: drums ('Moonchild')
Producer: David Gates
Studio: Sunset Sound Recorders, Hollywood, CA
Label: A&M
Release date: October 1984

Having established themselves on the local scene by playing covers of blues numbers, the band rapidly built a following. Their sound reflected the blues of the 1960s British Invasion, with inspiration from bands such as The Rolling Stones, The Animals, The Yardbirds and The Pretty Things. Many people thought Captain Beefheart and the Magic Band were British. The Howlin' Wolf covers – which dominated their act and can be heard in the live recording from the Avalon Ballroom – suited Don's vocal style. On the strength of their performances, the Magic Band were signed to A&M Records for a two single deal.

In 1965, they took their first steps into a recording studio and laid down five tracks. Four of these came out on the two A&M singles, and one languished in the vaults: undiscovered until the 1980s when this EP was released by first A&M then Edsel.

'Diddy Wah Diddy' b/ w 'Who Do You Think You're Fooling?' and 'Moonchild' b/w 'Frying Pan' were released as singles. Just think, if these tracks had received sufficient airplay, they might well have broken through, and this R&B version of Beefheart might've gone on to produce more in the same vein to rival The Rolling Stones, The Pretty Things and Downliners Sect. The Magic Band were good enough. But it wasn't to be.

'Diddy Wah Diddy' (Blake, Dixon, McDaniels)

This was selected from the five tracks recorded by A&M as being the most likely to be a hit. It was originally written by Blind Blake in 1929 as a ragtime blues titled 'Diddie Wa Diddie'. Willie Dixon adapted the music and lyric, adding a distinctive Bo Diddley riff and a rock-and-roll/R&B vibe for a single in 1956.

The Beefheart arrangement is much heavier, with a thumping bass. The track is reminiscent of British-Invasion R&B but has fuzz bass that gives it a punchier characteristic. Don's voice was greatly suited to this delivery, and his blues-harp-playing added a rich bluesy element. Unfortunately for Don and the boys, the Boston group The Remains released an adaptation of the song simultaneously. Synchronicity, huh? The Remains' version is also great, though not as heavy as Beefheart's. They probably undercut each other, so neither reached the national charts. The single became a local hit, but broke no further than that. If it had, things might've been different: perhaps they might've stuck with A&M and remained an R&B band, who knows? History turns on small events.

The song was later covered by many notable people, including Leon Redbone, Ry Cooder, Taj Mahal, The Sonics, The Blues Band and Manfred Mann.

'Who Do You Think You're Fooling?' (Van Vliet)
The B-side of the single is a self-penned upbeat number with that same heavy-bass R&B vibe. The lyric is quite straightforward and lacks that signature Van Vliet complex poetic touch. Don claimed it was about the government and the statue of liberty, but I'm not sure that comes across. To me, they seem more like a slightly misogynistic product of the day. Don is saying that this is a man's world. Don wanted to be boss.

'Moonchild' (Gates)
The second single was penned by the producer David Gates (of Bread fame), though it sounds much more like Don's writing style to me. It was recorded six months after the other tracks. Paul Blakely had returned, and Alex St. Clair moved back to guitar. It's a reprise of the R&B style, but this time with a haunting Yardbirds-like chorus. The predominant bass drives it along, with Don's voice powerful and clear. The song and arrangement are less straightforward than the other tracks, but it was certainly strong enough to be a hit. For some reason, it failed to chart, and the contract with A&M expired.

'Frying Pan' (Van Vliet)
The B-side is another Van Vliet number driven by a thumping R&B riff. Not quite as bassy as the previous two sides, there is more guitar riff and blues harp. Once again, the Captain's lyrics are quite straightforward, describing the end of a relationship and the struggle of trying to succeed. It's a powerful number that might not have been out of place on *Safe As Milk*.

'Here I Am I Always Am' (Van Vliet)
The final track is another Van Vliet original that lay hidden in the vaults, and was only half-remembered. It became a mythical beast until it was finally rediscovered in the 1980s. The lyrics are straightforward – following a bust-up, this is a simple plea for his girl to take him seriously; to not take his love in vain. A strange fast rhythm augments the R&B flavour, and the experimental tempo changes that transform the song into something more have a hint of what was to come later.

Safe As Milk (1967)

Personnel:
Don Van Vliet: vocals, harmonica, marimba
Alex St. Clair Snouffer: guitar, bass (9, 10), percussion
Jerry Handley: bass (except on 8, 9, 10)
Ry Cooder: guitar, slide guitar, bass (8), percussion
John French 'Drumbo': drums
Sam Hoffman: theremin (6, 12)
Russ Titelman: guitar
Richard Perry: harpsichord
Milt Holland: log drum, tambourine, percussion (2, 4, 8)
Taj Mahal: tambourine, percussion (7)
Studios: Sunset Sound; RCA
Producers: Richard Perry, Bob Krasnow
Engineer (and demos): Gary (Magic) Marker
Label: Buddah

This album is a very good entry point for those who are unfamiliar with the work of Captain Beefheart. Don had been listening to jazz musicians John Coltrane, Charles Mingus and Miles Davis, and had a clear vision for the way he wanted the band to go. He wanted to be more experimental and move away from straightforward blues to incorporate African rhythms and jazz, and take on the acid vibe of the day. However, that was a work in progress, and for this album, he retained the heavy blues base, which made it accessible to the uninitiated. This was still desert blues, but now with an acid tinge.

Much was happening in 1966. It was a watershed year of great change. The key factor was drugs. While marijuana and speed had been staple drugs for the blues/R&B vibe, there was now the sudden influx of LSD. It transformed the attitudes of the musicians and audiences. In England, this had an impact on established bands like The Yardbirds, the Stones, The Animals and The Pretty Things, who changed quite dramatically from straightforward bands playing Chicago blues, into experimental psychedelic bands. The process could be clearly seen with The Beatles' evolution on albums from *Please Please Me* to the psychedelic *Sgt. Pepper's Lonely Hearts Club Band*. Newer psychedelic bands like Pink Floyd and The Jimi Hendrix Experience were starting out just as a new underground venue scene sprang up to cater for them.

On America's West Coast, a new style of music labelled acid rock was emerging. Bands such as The Doors, Love, Jefferson Airplane, Big Brother and The Holding Company, Country Joe and The Fish and Grateful Dead were sweeping in. Beefheart was on the crest of this wave.

In order to achieve his new vision, Don knew that changes had to be made. Clearly, some of the band members – though well versed in the blues – were unable to make the transition to acid rock. The first to go was drummer Paul Blakely, who was replaced by John French (later named Drumbo). This was an important change because not only was John (incidentally, also from Lancaster) an accomplished drummer and master of the complex polyrhythms that Don was envisioning, but he could also read and transcribe music, so was able to interpret Don's ideas from his piano-playing, humming or singing, notating them and organising the band to play the music that was coming from Don's mind. This talent would become more and more important as the band developed, the music became more complex, and the Captain became stranger and stranger.

With John on board, the band moved to Los Angeles in order to break into the wider music arena and seek a record deal. The underground scene was beginning to take off with venues like the Avalon Ballroom, where they found their own specific type of audience. The second change, was to find a guitarist who could handle the more complex arrangements. Don had been impressed by the guitar-playing of young musician Ryland Cooder who was in a moderately successful folk/R&B band called The Rising Sons. Ry was a 20-year-old guitar/slide prodigy whose skills Don coveted. Don knew that Ry could transform the band's sound. However, what followed was – sadly – a game of intrigue and deception.

The Rising Sons comprised Taj Mahal and Ry on guitar and Gary 'Magic' Marker on bass. In order to lure Ry into his band, Don promised Gary Marker both the management of the band, and production of their new album. The ruse worked. Ry joined them and was the key to developing their sound and helping to arrange the more intricate songs. Ry's inclusion sparked the firing of guitarist Doug Moon, who couldn't get the hang of the new music. It nearly proved to be the end for Jerry Handley too. Session musicians were brought in to play some of the bass parts.

Unfortunately for Gary, things didn't work out as promised. The band recorded a number of demos with him, but just before they went into the RCA studios, he was demoted to sound engineer. Richard Perry took over. This was Perry's first job as a producer. (He went on to produce just about everybody from Ringo Starr to Carly Simon and Art Garfunkel, and is now revered). However, during this first project, he became overwhelmed with the complexities of the Beefheart album, and Bob Krasnow had to step in to complete the job. Ry was not impressed with the final result, feeling that the album should've been completely remixed. This would've been difficult because Richard had combined many of the tracks together into a single one.

Interestingly, there still exists an unreleased acetate of some of the Gary Marker demos, including a couple of R&B versions of blues tracks (perhaps recorded live at the Avalon Ballroom), and Howlin' Wolf and Chuck Berry numbers: neither of which appear on the later album.

Not only had the band's music developed, but the lyrics had also taken a leap forward. Of the 12 tracks, 11 were originals. The one blues cover was 'Grown So Ugly' by Louisiana blues musician Robert Pete Williams. A number of the tracks were written in an abstract poetic style: a move on from the straightforward lyrics of the A&M sessions. Eight of the 12 tracks were co-written with one Herb Bermann, though nothing was known of this mythical figure for many years. People claim to have been introduced to three different people, all of whom were supposed to be Herb Bermann. Don once said that he was fictional and was created just to confuse the publishers. Herb Bermann was a poet living in the Lancaster region. He later emerged from the shadows and claimed to have written all of this album's lyrics. Truth can be stranger than fiction. Certainly, the tracks attributed to Herb Bermann are different and generally superior to the others. Was the hype around Bermann another twist of the Captain's rich imagination and his desire to create mystery? The relationship with this desert poet certainly seemed to alter Don's approach to poetic lyric writing, as his following work displays a unique and surreal quality.

Ry found recording the album to be a traumatic experience, and after playing a gig in which the Captain – high on acid and claiming to have seen a girl in the audience morph into a fish, blowing bubbles out of her mouth – adjusted his tie and stepped off the ten-foot-high stage and landed on Bob Krasnow, Ry decided to leave the band. He'd found it impossible to work with Don and called him 'a music Nazi', although he was impressed with Don's musical ideas, and thought *Safe As Milk* was an incredible album, even if badly mixed. Nevertheless, the album had been recorded, changes made, and the band was moving forward.

There are various stories about the record's label Buddah. The band's first label A&M rejected the demos outright after hearing 'Electricity' – they were horrified by what they considered to be vulgar lyrics, and immediately severed all links with the band. Beefheart had become far too weird for them! Apparently, demos were hawked around many places before Buddah finally gave the band the go-ahead.

Originally the album title was to be Abba-Zaba – a chewy taffy candy bar with a creamy peanut butter centre and a distinctive yellow-and-black-checked wrapper. The candy bar manufacturers were not keen on being associated with Beefheart. The album title was changed, but the characteristic yellow-and-black checks were retained for the cover. The title *Safe As Milk* was generally thought to be an allusion to LSD properties, and was a statement that immediately connected to the underground audience Don was seeking.

The album was released in 1967, at the forefront of the acid rock revolution crashing out of West Coast, USA. In 1970 when Buddah's distribution passed to Polydor, they reissued it on their budget Pye Marble Arch label cut from 12 tracks to ten, omitting 'I'm Glad' and 'Grown So Ugly'). A further reissue on the Buddah label in Polydor's budget 99 series was in stereo for the first time, with the title changed to *Dropout Boogie*: firstly, as a ten-track and then with the two missing tracks reinstated. The 1999 CD release, on Sony's correctly spelt Buddha label, features all twelve tracks plus seven bonus tracks from the sessions of the proposed partially live follow-up album *The Mirror Man*.

I can still remember the thrill of Mike playing me that album. The acid-drenched desert blues jiggled my brain cells with delight. I hadn't heard anything like it before.

'Sure 'Nuff 'N Yes I Do' (Van Vliet, Bermann)

The opening track of my Beefheart journey begins with a piece of solo blues slide guitar courtesy of Ry Cooder. The electric guitar sounds as sharp as a diamond and progresses into rhythmic mode as Don's rich voice begins. That first line stolen straight from 'New Minglewood Blues' by the Noah Lewis Jug Band tells a fictional story of Don's life, giving it a mystical twist of Dali-esque magic – a modern-day bragging bluesman. He was born in the desert, but came from the voodoo of New Orleans, whipped up by a tornado, imbued with the magic of the Sun and Moon.

The band kicks in with thumping bass, a driving guitar riff and a complex drum rhythm. The background slide creates a characteristic duelling guitar sound that transforms the song into a masterpiece that's no longer blues but a unique guitar-driven heavy rock number with a catchy chorus. Man, this cat had everything a girl needed, From flashy cars to a surefire brand of loving. Sleep with him and he'd sure teach you something, Sure enough 'n' yes he would.

This wasn't blues and it wasn't psychedelia. It was Beefheart: acid blues straight out of the Mojave Desert.

'Zig Zag Wanderer' (Van Vliet, Bermann)

No sooner has the desert dust settled than we are zigzagging through another epic, as Don – just like the three pigs – has a house that the big bad wolf can't blow down. That house is a metaphor for the mystical elements of nature and the planet. Don's aim was to stomp, prance, wander and dance his way around the world: sating his thirst on adventure.

The track starts with a drum and guitar refrain ending with a gong and the hushed voice announcing 'zig zag'. Immediately we're into a guitar-driven riff and heavy bass pattern with Don exclaiming the joys of zigging and zagging. The song is built around a repetitive hypnotic riff terminating in a warbling voice and change of rhythm. Background vocals and rhythmic changes maintain the interest, with the riff building to a climax at the end of each verse. The guitars drop out as Don delivers his vocal on a slower section based around a repeating drum roll and complex bass line. Then the guitars cut back in, taking the song to its climax, terminating in that gong again and the hushed 'zig zag'. Zig-Zag was a popular cigarette paper for rolling joints.

This is the first of Don's mystical environmental paeans. Life is a joy. We have to dance our way through it and take care of nature on the way. We're all zig-zag wanderers.

'Call On Me' (Van Vliet)

'Call On Me' calms the tempo a little. Without Bermann's poetic influence it's a straightforward classic love song minus surreal imagery or intricacy. When you are lonely and blue, you can call on the Captain, who is always there to give you love. You can trust him.

The song is still heavy – based around a blues structure, with a soulful vocal delivery, some great drumming patterns and rhythm changes. We get to hear some of the higher reaches of Don's fantastic vocal range.

'Dropout Boogie' (Van Vliet, Bermann)

'Dropout Boogie' aims straight at the heart of the anti-establishment underground subculture. Don's harsh vocal ridicules the establishment's mantra – work hard at school, get a job, get married, settle down and become a brick in the pillar of society. Don's message is to drop out: very powerful, and certainly resonates with the attitude of the time. It hit the zeitgeist right between the eyes, paralleling Don's own experience with education while also starting the wordplay that we'll see later: 'adapt her, adapter'.

The track has a heavy repetitive riff. The powerful fuzz guitar and distorted voice start the song; words pumping out in a punchy, growly snarl. Then follows an instrumental middle eight with a rhythm change to waltz time – an unusual light marimba-based interlude, before the fuzz guitars thud back in and the insistent vocals return.

'I'm Glad' (Van Vliet)

We're back into another mundane lyric in a rather ordinary love song – no pyrotechnics, metaphor or lysergic twist, just a standard love song. Though sung soulfully, this is little more than a slow, mundane ballad with a backing of girl singers, verging on doo-wop. I can see why it was dropped from the album's ten-track version. Although beautiful and competently delivered, it's by no means an acid rock blues number. It would be more at home on a 1950s R&B album. But hey, that voice really shines.

'Electricity' (Van Vliet, Bermann)

Here we are thrown into the ultimate acid-drenched Bermann poetry, for what is the quintessential early Beefheart song:

> Singin' through you to me
> Thunderbolts caught easily
> Shouts the truth peacefully
> Electricity

I remember Don's incredible voice roaring this in live performance, rippling your eardrums. 'Electricity' was like a clarion call to the new age.

The song starts with electric guitar, simple bass and cymbals in the background, quickly moving into weird slide-guitar notes. The Captain sings the opening three lines quietly over slide guitar, before launching into the slightly distorted and elongated roar of 'Eeeeleeeectriiiiiicityyyy': so powerfully delivered, it's reputed to have blown the mic. A bass line sets the rhythm, and the band kicks in, drums and bass creating a pulsating rhythm. The guitar riff repeats, with a theremin overlaying a long clear throbbing note, giving a sci-fi feel. The track pounds along. A double-tracked Don alternating between normal and slightly distorted verses creates a kind of duelling: effective early use of stereo panning.

This song is so powerful. The lyric is about bringing light to the world: a lighthouse beacon pointing the way. At the time, acid was seen as the electricity that illuminates the brain on the quest for self-discovery.

The track finishes with an unearthly undulating theremin note, with a few beeps at the end: reminiscent of a space satellite. The Bermann lyric coupled with the innovative, experimental theremin sounds create a transcendental track that at the time was highly original and frightening enough to scare off A&M Records. What a song to close the first side. It became a regular in live performance.

'Yellow Brick Road' (Van Vliet, Bermann)

Side two starts with a single note. Then producer Richard Perry announces, 'The following tone is a reference tone operating at our recording level'. The note rises to a spacey weirdness before the guitar enters, quickly followed by the rest of the band. It's an upbeat number, driven along by the snare drum patterns and slide guitar riffs. The jaunty feel is evident in Bermann's lyric.

The slide guitar is deployed in an unusual way. Coupled with the snare in the other channel, it sets a fast rhythmic foundation for the Captain to sing over.

These were the early days of the positive 1960s vibe. Flower power and love-ins were the antidote to the establishment's warmongering and grey conformity. The poem shows the singer discovering the power of love and following the magical yellow brick road into a world of colour, fun and joy; the 'tricks and candy sticks' being the LSD passport to a world of psychedelic wonder. The lyric's naivety matched the mood of the day. The Beatles were singing 'All You Need Is Love'. This was the start of an era of love and peace. We were going to change the world, and the vision of that colourful future was laid out in this early Beefheart song.

'Abba Zaba' (Van Vliet)

This is the first song that really shows the impact of Herb Bermann's poetry on Don's writing. It's a surreal epic of crazy images, reminiscent of Herb's work.

Abba Zaba go-zoom Babbette baboon
Run, run, monsoon, Indian dream, tiger moon
Yellow bird fly high, tobacco sky, two shadows at noon

Making sense of the surreal poetic imagery is challenging. I used to think it was about evolution and the arrogance of man, represented as a baboon silhouetted against the sky, but I might well have been wrong. It's named after the Abba Zaba café that Don used to frequent, and certainly, the baboon is a reference to the ape that the young Don used to visit in the observatory zoo. That ape makes a number of appearances in future songs. Perhaps the Dali-esque imagery should just stand as it is. Perhaps there is no meaning. In any case, it's a classic. It has everything in terms of music and imagery and was the song both Don and later the Magic Band played live most frequently.

Following Drumbo's drum rhythm, the Captain is in the left channel, Ry's guitar is playing a catchy riff on the right with the bass in the background. You can clearly hear what John 'Drumbo' French brings to the sound. His rhythms are intricate and varied, with the African feel Don was so keen on. The song is complex, with changes in tempo and dynamic. A bass solo from Ry is quite a collector's item, and the chorus has an infectious hook. What more could you want?

'Plastic Factory' (Van Vliet, Bermann, Handley)

This song has Bermann lyrics, but a simpler orthodox structure and the meaning is transparent. Jerry Handley has a co-writing credit, but he doesn't actually play bass on the track.

It's quite apparent that Don disliked the polluting technology and plastic way of life that society created. The song's sentiments remind me of Jimmy Reed's 'Big Boss Man'. Don craves a life more in tune with nature. The factory is no place for him.

The song is in a more-bluesy style, with the Captain's blues harp carrying it along. The band creates a churning rhythm, with the Captain delivering the lyric in a voice full of deep resonance, rising to a high trill at the end of each line, to create emphasis. That voice, with its characteristic lift became a trademark. The instrumental middle eight breaks the mood with a sudden change of tempo and rhythm to 12/8. Don's squeaky harmonica is reminiscent of Jimmy Reed's, but the complex rhythm changes take the song beyond that of a standard blues number, and are prescient of what was to come on *Trout Mask Replica*.

'Where There's Woman' (Van Vliet, Bermann)

This song was a Don and Herb collaboration, but has a more orthodox structure than some of their joint efforts. A poem based around simple rhymes, results in a straightforward love song. The lyric suggests that in a world of lies and evil, there is good, love and peace. Music is the vehicle, and the good Captain will provide sweet honey-wine loving. This slow moody piece has a swampy guitar, interesting drum and bongo rhythms and a deep bluesy vocal with characteristic rises full of nuance and aching emotion. The number suddenly speeds up at the chorus, with a fast tempo call-and-response between the band and Don.

'Grown So Ugly' (Robert Pete Williams)

This is the album's only cover song, which was unexpected because the band was still performing a lot of blues numbers by Howlin' Wolf, Blind Willie Johnson and John Lee Hooker etc.. The song was included at Ry's insistence. He coaxed Don into singing it and arranged it for the album.

I can see why the Captain was attracted to Robert Pete Williams, who had a unique guitar-playing style using interesting staccato rhythms: not the usual thing. Robert's original was an excellent acoustic version telling the tale of the ageing process – getting so old and ugly that you don't even recognise yourself in the mirror, and your woman doesn't know who you are.

Beefheart and the band transformed the song into a pounding heavy electrified number with a churning guitar riff. Don's voice hits high notes displaying his vocal range. The song has a couple of rhythm changes and a middle eight with a change of dynamic. The pared-back sound is based around that single guitar and the Captain's anguished voice. Very powerful.

Autumn's Child (Van Vliet, Bermann)

The album ends with the track that probably has the most musical variety, interspersing gentle guitar and cymbals with punchy choruses, slow shuffles and fast pounding sections. Some sections teem with instruments, while others have very few. The weird spacey theremin once again adds a futuristic dimension. Don's vocal also ranges from soft and gentle to fierce and strong.

The lyric is one of Bermann's surreal ones, though maybe not quite as impervious as some.

> Apples shine share together
> Got the time to make her mine
> Fish pond streaks love kind
> Found the child I had to find

The words describe the end of summer, newly discovered love and pastoral delights. The doom-laden chorus exhorts us to 'go back ten years ago' with 'the sunbeams dancing round': suggesting that this idyllic relationship was in the past. A sad song of love lost.

Re-released as *The File Series* (Pye International, 1977): a double album with *Mirror Man*.
Re-released as *Music in Sea Minor* (Buddah, 1983): 6 tracks from *Safe As Milk* and two from *Mirror Man*).
Re-released as the picture disc *Top Secret* (Design, 1984): 6 tracks from *Safe As Milk*, plus '25th Century Quaker' from *Mirror Man*.
Re-released as *Abba Zaba* (Masters, 1988): 6 tracks from *Safe As Milk*, plus '25th Century Quaker' from *Mirror Man*.
Re-released as Captain Beefheart at His Best (Special Music Company, 1989)

Re-released as Zig Zag Wanderer (Object Enterprises, 1991)
Re-released as The Best Beefheart (Buddah, 1988): ith 'Kandy Korn', '25th Century Quaker' and *'Mirror Man'* from *Strictly Personal*.

Bonus tracks on the 1999 CD release (Addressed in the *Mirror Man* Sessions section, where they belong):
'Safe As Milk' (take 5) (Don Van Vliet), 'On Tomorrow' (Don Van Vliet), 'Big Black Baby Shoes' (Don Van Vliet), 'Flower Pot' (Don Van Vliet), 'Dirty Blue Gene' (Don Van Vliet), 'Trust Us' (take 9) (Don Van Vliet), 'Korn Ring Finger' (Don Van Vliet)

Mirror Man (1971)

Personnel:
Captain Beefheart: vocal, harmonica, oboe, shehnai
Alex St. Clair Snouffer: guitar
Jeff Cotton aka 'Antennae' Jimmy Semens: guitar
Jerry Handley: bass
John French 'Drumbo': drums
Studio: TTG, Hollywood, CA
Producer: Bob Krasnow
Label: Buddah

The loss of Ry Cooder was huge. He'd arranged all the music on *Safe As Milk* and had taken the band to another level. Ry was replaced by Jeff Cotton – another young guitarist from the Lancaster area – who the Captain later renamed 'Antennae' Jimmy Semens. John French stepped up and became the arranger, teacher and interpreter.

The Magic Band had a harder, dirtier sound than other bands, partly due to the steel picks they attached to their fingers. The picks were usually used by pedal-steel players, and Gerry McGee suggested them to the band.

Mirror Man was conceived as a double album with the name *It Comes To You In A Plain Brown Wrapper*. One album was to be recorded live, capturing the psychedelic blues of their stage act, although this was not actually recorded in front of a live audience but as a studio jam. Don intended the other album to comprise studio-recorded songs following on in the same vein as *Safe As Milk*.

This was a transitional album, between the delta blues of their early performances and the psychedelic poetry and music of their acid rock. Don had clearly seen the power of Herb Bermann's poetry and Ry's musical arrangements. At the time, LSD was having a huge impact on the underground scene, and Don was a devotee. He was a highly creative person with an experimental nature. The acid, poetry and the underground scene, in general, were having a dramatic effect on his neural connections. A nuclear fusion was going on in his cortex, and with everything rewired, his eccentricity became even more pronounced. He started blending his poetry, the blues, African rhythms and free-form jazz into something else: a peyote/mescalin-drenched gumbo/soup of nuclear desert blues – not surprising, really, as John French remembers that before doing the sessions, their tea was spiked with LSD.

When it was finally released four years later, *Mirror Man* – with its long hypnotic jams – rapidly gained a reputation as being the ideal stoner album. The Buddah executives didn't know what to make of these long rambling tracks. They were of the opinion that the album wasn't commercially viable and was thus unsuitable as a follow-up to *Safe As Milk*. They pulled the plug on the project, leaving the band high and dry with hours of unfinished material and no release.

'Tarotplane' (Van Vliet, Johnson, Johnson, Dixon)

Captain Beefheart and the band had all been fully immersed in the blues, and played in blues bands, some together in Lancaster. They were not only familiar with the delta blues of the likes of Son House and Blind Willie Johnson but also the more-electric Chicago blues of Howlin' Wolf. As blues musicians, they were used to jamming. 'Tarotplane' shows them extending the number, incorporating a psychedelic feel, transforming and updating the song. Don was able to sing over the top of this, combining lyrics from specific blues numbers with a few of his own more-surreal words.

The name and some of the lyrics came from the 1936 Robert Johnson song 'Terraplane Blues'. Don changed it to 'Tarotplane', giving that 1960s mystical edge. Tarot cards, the I Ching and other spiritual concepts were a popular counterculture element, along with Eastern mysticism and Buddhist philosophy. A song originally written about a 1930s car becomes a journey into a different dimension: a flight into space.

The 19-minute jam settles into a heavy bass-driven churn, sounding like a freight train gathering momentum. The sound is a little muddy, but the rhythm guitar on the left channel vies with the slide guitar on the right. The Captain plays some brilliant harp over the top, and after a minute, he comes in with the vocal. He starts with an adaptation of Blind Willie Johnson's 'You're Gonna Need Somebody On Your Bond', the intro updating the words 'Baby Percy told Elixir Sue....'. He's playing with words: 'Mice in the radiator/Razors in the clay'. The drums are playing some intricate rhythms, the guitars and bass rumbling along with variations on the riffs. It's spellbinding. The Captain blows a bit on the shehnai (given to him by Ornette Coleman), adding a discordant element. Don throws in sections of Howlin' Wolf's Willie Dixon-written classic 'Wang Dang Doodle', then comes back to Robert Johnson's 'Terraplane'. There's not much variation in the music, just a groove that draws you relentlessly on. Don alternates between the Willie Johnson, Willie Dixon and Robert Johnson, throwing out verses, adding a few of his own and telling his girl that she's gonna fly. At the end, there are a few rhythm changes coupled with high, piercing, discordant notes: a forewarning of what's to come when he really gets going on *Trout Mask Replica*.

Quite a journey!! 19 minutes seems to go by just like that.

'Kandy Korn' (Van Vliet)

Is this song – like 'Abba Zaba' – about confectionary? Or is it – as many of the underground freaks supposed – about the multi-coloured lysergic acid pills? We'll never know. But there sure are some bright colours! It starts with the Captain intoning an elongated 'Yellow and orange', with the band providing discordant backing vocals. Then the music gallops in. The first couple of minutes are the vocal section with Don extolling the virtues of yellow and orange candy corn – so good he wants to eat them; to be reborn, reformed, stay warm. Sounds like acid to me!

There are some great bass lines, coupled with double-tracked vocals. The track then settles into a long instrumental phase. At first, the guitars are a little hidden in the mix, with the drums very much to the fore. The jam settles into a rhythm. There are a few backing vocals, but in general, the drumming leads, with a heavy underlying bass as guitars lock together in intricate phrases. The piece builds and progresses with the guitars making circling melodies. Phew – 8 minutes of psychedelic joy! Gimme some of that Kandy Korn!!

'25th Century Quaker' (Van Vliet)

The Captain was toying with starting a band called 25th Century Quakers. They even played some gigs under that name, and Don persuaded them to dress in black Quaker robes. That must've been fun: quite an image.

This is another ten-minute jam starting with a thumping bass line, some oboe-playing from the Captain, John's heavy drum rhythm and the guitars picking up the rhythm and melody. Don's vocal sounds as if he's jamming with words, making them up, adapting them, using rhymes and word association to create an acid-soaked scene. He describes faces melting into blue cheese, and sunlight passing from him to us as he walks through the cottage with his girl; 25th-century Quakers linking to the Mayflower; eyes fluttering like wide-open shutters on to this world of flowers and wonder. It's a trip in words and music.

The band's supreme musicianship enables the interchange of ideas, playing off each other in a fluid manner, developing themes punctuated by also sax interjections. The Captain's vocals – more pronounced than on the other tracks – is loose and free. We're all spiritual explorers on a trip into the future – a world full of sunshine, flowers and love – and the Captain is a conduit for the power of the universe; the band an expression of that flow.

'Mirror Man' (Van Vliet)

Probably the most complex and fully developed of the album's four jams, this long jam settles into a scintillating groove. Don liked playing with the sound of words. The phrase '*Mirror Man*' is a good example, being extended, distorted and transformed into 'mere man'.

It starts with a snatch of Don's harmonica, the slide guitar then establishing the groove. Heavy drums provide an intricate pattern that persists throughout the track's 15 minutes. This is what John 'Drumbo' French brought to the band – superb powerful drumming, fabulous rhythms that never become tedious, and a relentless power that drives the whole jam along. With the guitars interchanging lead, slide and rhythm in amazing patterns, everything seems to be going 'round and 'round in interconnecting circles that tap directly into your cortex. The Captain's powerful vocals play with both sound and rhythm, distort words, invent absurd rhymes and descend into guttural sounds that break up and are propelled out at you like aural bullets. The funky groove sets your whole body rocking and every cell lurching. The music ebbs and flows, building to a climax as the vocal returns and captures you. We're peering into the Captain's surreal mirror, from which a whole other universe is reflected.

Don intended these four long, live jams to make up one of the albums in the double set, without any further overdubbing or editing. He wanted them raw. The other album of shorter studio tracks – more of a follow-on from *Safe As Milk* – demonstrates the other side of Beefheart with poetry and musical exploration. That album remains unfinished. Some tracks had been recorded, some remaining only half-realised. They sat in the vaults, abandoned and untouched for 24 years.

Contemporary Recordings
I May Be Hungry But I Sure Ain't Weird (1992)
Label: Sequel Records
Recorded in 1967 at TTG studios with the personnel from the Mirror Man album (Originally It Comes To You In A Plain Brown Wrapper).
In 1992, Sequel Records came to an arrangement with Buddha to release outtakes from the *Mirror Man* sessions. We knew of these fabled tracks (intended to be half of the It Comes To You In A Plain Brown Wrapper album), but we'd never heard them. Apparently, Don had been furious about Bob Krasnow's production of the *Strictly Personal* album, but this album was reputed to contain the original recordings: the raw tracks as the Captain had initially intended.

So it was with great trepidation that I first played this album. Was it going to be as good as I'd imagined? Well not really. I love *Strictly Personal*, and don't mind the phasing or psychedelic gimmickry at all. The tracks on *I May Be Hungry But I Sure Ain't Weird*give us a glimpse into the sessions and what the band sounded like without all the psychedelic production, and that is interesting. Some tracks are better; some are worse. Some are fully formed; a number of them are incomplete (lacking vocals and overdubs). It's a mixed bag. A great album, though.

'Trust Us' (Take 6) (Van Vliet)
The opener is a fully-fledged psychedelic masterpiece beginning with a sustained drum rhythm and soft guitar; Don gently recites lyrics in an expressive manner. The song gradually builds, with chiming guitar, drums and bass creating a hypnotic rhythm. The vocal becomes a powerful force. The track includes characteristic changing rhythms, circling musical refrains and storming crescendos that plateau before receding. The changes of pace create tension. With elongations and distortions, Don's voice generates a punchy section of repeated words and the motif 'Let the dyin' die, let the lyin' lie!', which fades to the end.

Don's poem is a spiritual exploration of life. He delves into the zeitgeist of the moment with its search for truth, purpose and spiritual rebirth. He implores us to trust him and to look within and find a better way – to live, to see, to feel, to love; not to fall into the ways of greed and destruction. Let the old ways die. Let the old live their empty lives. Youth will have its day and flourish. The band is the harbinger of a better way of living.

'Beatle Bones N' Smokin' Stones (Part 1)' (Van Vliet)
A homage to (or mockery) of The Beatles and the Stones (?). The poem is reminiscent of the Bermann style – bizarre and obscure, fractured and stuffed with imagery: coloured sunsets, soft cracker bats and Cheshire cats. Don is playing with ideas, rhythms and free-form association. The psychedelic world of Sgt. Pepper's... is a playground for Don to flow through on a lysergic romp, using words that may sound like nonsense but actually play with subtle meanings, such as 'Strawberry feels forever': a surreal play-on-words. Don writes about life and death, implying that as the dry sand falls, we become bones. Living creatures are cellular sailboats on the oceans of life. We've seen and loved and feel forever.

Starting with a bluesy picked guitar, the Captain sings – his voice intertwining with the guitar: rising, falling, distorting, soaked with expression. The music pauses and restarts, interspersed with tempo changes; the band provides a heavy rhythm. The poem is sung beautifully and is fully enclosed in the music. The bass slides prominently, and then gives way to quiet passages with twiddling guitars. 'Who are dark? Who are day?'. Experimental, extraordinary, a perfect melding of vocal and music.

'Moody Liz' (Take 8) (Van Vliet, Bermann)
A song of two halves. The first section is unusual for a Beefheart number, having dreamy vocals, soft singing and vocal harmonies. The poetic Bermann lyrics are weird and obscure. The poem was originally entitled 'Wee Little Doors' – a nonsense verse put together for the rhyme and sound rather than sense. 'Her lunar spoon, croon a tune', 'Babble clabber streams'.

The second longer section settles into a typical Beefheart track. The drums are prominent and the composition is based around the two duelling guitars. The guitars each have a unique tone and texture, playing individual developing riffs yet melding, weaving and gelling together before pulling apart.

It's a compelling number, but to me, it feels incomplete. I keep expecting a Beefheart vocal to be laid over it, though there is none on any other take. Perhaps Don was never happy enough with the backing track to record a vocal. Or perhaps this is exactly what he intended. Hard to say.

'Safe As Milk' (Take 12) (Van Vliet)
A quirky accessible song with a catchy melody and plenty of variation. Don's vocal is fluid, powerful, and gels perfectly with the flow of the complex song.

It starts with the full band crashing in and continues apace. Drums and guitars are loud, bass a little deeper in the mix, slide guitar picking runs as the rhythm guitar drives the pace. The chorus has a different feel, finished off with the whooping voice. The perfect singing is double-tracked and powerful. Later, the slide guitar repeats a note over the rhythm guitar motif. It ends with a heavy resonating bass tone, the guitarists' high notes twiddling down on the bridge.

The lyrics spill forth with acid poetry; Don's tripping observations of spiders spinning webs, strange newspaper headlines and the moldering contents of his fridge. The vocal ends with the announcement that he may be hungry, but he sure ain't weird. Don was ambitious. He knew what he was doing; not just being weird for the sake of being weird. There is substance here. The music has gravitas. He was right!

'Gimme Dat Harp Boy' (Van Vliet)
Another blues groove based around an infectious guitar riff and bass line. Like a wild throbbing heartbeat with wailing harp and gutsy vocals, this was written after seeing a Canned Heat performance. Don was curious to see the competition but was not impressed with Bob Hite's vocal and harp performance: 'Gimme that harp boy/It ain't no fat man's toy'. He kept asking why Canned Heat were playing all those 'dead peoples' music. Don thought that to play the blues, a musician had to add their own style and take it up a notch. 'Gimme Dat Harp Boy' demonstrated how that could be done. The song is futuristic acid blues straight out of the swampy desert, if you can have a swampy desert.

'Harp toke, harp smoke, harp float' – this number propels us into another dimension. It's stoned blues for the futuristic children of the 1960s revolution – blues for tomorrow. Don's harp-playing demonstrates that he was a master of the instrument.

'On Tomorrow' (Instrumental) (Van Vliet)
An instrumental that was intended to be a backing track, but no vocals were ever added. Yet, having sufficient innovation and punch, this can stand on its own. There are no gimmicks or fancy production techniques, and the instruments are clearly separated. The complex guitar interchanges and rhythms are laid bare. This makes it a fascinating track because the piece's structure is fully revealed, unobscured by a vocal.

The opening section has an oriental sound, but the whole piece has the feel of jazz improvisation. However, the music is all carefully choreographed – even the cymbals and weird guitar noises in the pared-back sections, which sound very much like free-form jazz. The result is a compulsive piece that finishes with a climax of drums, bass and chopping rhythm guitar before fading away.

'Trust Us' (Take 9) (Van Vliet)
This is a fully realised song with overdubs resulting in a very different feel to that of take 6, which started this album. This begins with dreamy backing vocals and soft guitar; the Captain reciting the first lines in a gentle tone. The track has all the elements of take 6 but is slower, more subdued and moody.

27

Here the drums are further back in the mix, and guitars are softer and less immediate. Though still containing the long, sustained notes, short drum solo and extended outro, this softer approach creates a very different ambience. I like them both, but if pushed, prefer the harder tone of take 6.

'Safe As Milk' (Take 5) (Van Vliet)
I certainly like this mix as much as take 12, but it is different. There's an emphasis on other instruments. The drums set up a driving rhythm, the left channel guitar is nicely to the fore and the bass lays down a fast, steady throb.

A number of the instruments are panned to the right channel. There is little separation. The rhythm guitar could be sharper and more distinct. The music has been roughly mixed and everything shoved on to the one track, which is why the separation of instruments is so poor. Nonetheless, the melding guitars work for me and I love that sustained note over the drum rolls and the twiddling guitars for the extended fade.

'Big Black Baby Shoes' (Instrumental) (Van Vliet)
A short but interesting instrumental that starts with the bass and guitar in unison and then veers off into a range of phases and tempos. The guitar follows a pleasant melody with a simple backing of bass and drums. The rhythms and intermeshing guitars are light and accessible. This could even be a pop song.

'Flower Pot' (Instrumental) (Van Vliet)
The title itself resonates because this was the time of what the media called flower power, and pot was the sacrament of the age. Was the Captain putting the title's two words together as a send-up? I guess we'll never know. Oh, for some lyrics.

This instrumental starts with gentle guitars. The drums and bass start in the background and are brought forward in the mix to produce a swaying, lurching rhythm. As it progresses, the music speeds up with a change in rhythm and a great bubbling bass. Going along with a steady rhythm and repeating riff with variations that sound improvised but probably weren't, the track generates power. After reverting to the lurching riff near the end of the track, all the other instruments fade away to leave just the drumming.

'Dirty Blue Gene' (Instrumental) (Van Vliet)
This instrumental has nothing to do with Don's song 'Dirty Blue Gene' on Doc At The Radar Station. He must've liked the title and decided to recycle it. He did that with many things.

Starting at a slow, monotonous pace, it plods along into a hypnotic rhythm. It breaks into different rhythms and tempos but fails to develop into anything special.

This music eventually became 'Ice Rose' on Doc At The Radar Station. In the meantime, it went through a number of incarnations, as heard on the *The Spotlight Kid* outtakes.

The Mirror Man Sessions (1999)

The Buddha label (now renamed with correct spelling) finally released a CD of the *Mirror Man* sessions. The album contained the original four tracks (in a different order) along with an extra five tracks, all of which had been released on the 1992 *I May Be Hungry But I Sure Ain't Weird* album.

'Trust Us' (Take 6) (Van Vliet), 'Safe As Milk' (Take 12) (Van Vliet), 'Beatle Bones N' Smokin' Stones' (Van Vliet), 'Moody Liz' (Take 8) (Van Vliet), 'Gimme Dat Harp Boy' (Van Vliet)

Bonus tracks on the 1999 *Safe As Milk* CD

The 1999 *Safe As Milk* CD included seven more tracks from the *Mirror Man* sessions – those remaining from *I May Be Hungry But I Sure Ain't Weird*, plus 'Korn Ring Finger': the inclusion of which completed the release of all the *Mirror Man* sessions material.

'Safe As Milk' (Take 5) (Van Vliet), 'On Tomorrow' (Van Vliet), 'Big Black Baby Shoes' (Van Vliet), 'Flower Pot' (Van Vliet), 'Dirty Blue Gene' (Van Vliet), 'Trust Us' (Take 9) (Van Vliet)

'Korn Ring Finger' (Don Van Vliet)

This seven-minute track is a slow-dirge blues jam more in keeping with the four studio jams that formed the original *Mirror Man* album. The track was never properly recorded, and this feels like an early version with the band still feeling their way, even though some of the drumming is amazing. The result is splintered and restrained until the bass asserts itself. The vocal is set back in the mix. After five minutes, it picks up pace. Towards the end, everything drops out except for guitar and sparse blues harp. The band then returns for the outro: the Captain warbling in the background. The lyrics are poetic, fragmentary and druggy:

> In the hand of a funny little man
> Smokin' on golden cane
> Korn ring n' finger

The references to golden sunset and diamond stars of night, and the band blowin' and a brown paper bag, make it feel like a pot song. The Captain is enjoying playing with words.

The Sundazed label released some of these tracks on the 2008 vinyl album *It Comes To You In A Brown Paper Bag*, but did not meet the album's original concept. 'Moody Liz' (Take 16) has never been released anywhere else.

Strictly Personal (1968)

Personnel:
Don Van Vliet: vocals, harmonica
Jeff 'Antennae Jimmy Semens' Cotton: guitar
Alex 'St. Clair' Snouffer: guitar
Jerry Handley: bass
John 'Drumbo' French: drums
Producer: Bob Krasnow
Engineers: Gene Shiveley, Bill Lazerus
Studio: Sunset Sound Recorders, Hollywood, 25 April-2 May 1968
Art director: Tom Wilkes
Photography: Guy Webster
Label: Blue Thumb

I was an eager 19-year-old greatly anticipating the follow-up to *Safe As Milk*, completely unaware of what was taking place with Buddah and the recording of It Comes To You In A Plain Brown Wrapper. I knew nothing of Buddah's dumping of the band, or the following intrigue with Bob Krasnow's purloining of the tapes and setting up the Blue Thumb label. As far as I was concerned, the band were recording the *Safe As Milk* sequel, and I was hoping it would turn out to be just as brilliant. I was not disappointed. I loved it.

After Buddah had rejected the material, Bob Krasnow – clearly recognising the potential of the songs – set up his Blue Thumb label and signed the band. Here the story becomes murky. There are different accounts. One has Krasnow walking off with the Buddah tapes and merely remixing a number of them while perhaps re-recording a few. Another has the band re-recording all the tracks for Krasnow. Most probably, he did use a few from the Buddah recordings, remixing them and re-recording the rest.

Bob later returned the tapes to Buddah, and they finally released the bulk of that material on *Mirror Man*, The *Mirror Man* Sessions, and as bonus tracks on the *Safe As Milk* CD. I wonder if anything else worth hearing has been left in the vaults.

The album's second controversy was over how it had been mixed. Bob Krasnow – with an eye on the burgeoning psychedelic market and latest techniques – decided to use the phasing and reverb that was popular at the time: indeed, cutting edge, as deployed by The Beatles on their Revolver album. But here again, there are conflicting views. The band have stated that Don was complicit in the application of these effects, and only later claimed to be furious, saying that Bob Krasnow had completely ruined the project by drenching it with gimmicks. The band reported that Don only came out with that following poor sales and reviews. Personally, I can't see Bob having done anything without the knowledge and consent of Van Vliet (credited with arranging on the album), who was merely making excuses for the album's disappointing reception. Accounts from various sources have Don at the mixing board, so it may well have been Don himself playing around with the effects and later using Bob as a scapegoat.

The third controversy is over the songwriting. Don is credited with writing all the songs, but Herb Bermann states that he had a hand in writing a number of them: namely 'Safe As Milk', 'Trust Us', 'Kandy Korn' and 'Gimme Dat Harp Boy'. Nothing is ever straightforward with the Captain.

So, to the album. The front cover is quite interesting and sheds some light on a few things. It's not a brown paper bag; the concept has moved to become a mail package. This package contains material that is highly personal: a message from Captain Beefheart to his devotees. All the band members are represented as stamps. The addresses are also of note:

25th Century Quaker
One Ray Gun Drive
Celestial, Plainees

Capt. Beefheart & His Magic Band
5000/mgs. Tubular Falls Estates
Glassdom, Glassdom

We're back to the '25th Century Quaker' idea. We're now all 25th-century Quakers: special followers of this new cult. We live in the sci-fi region of One Ray Gun Drive, somewhere in the future on the spiritual celestial plains. Captain Beefheart & his Magic Band are sending us a highly confidential and spiritual missive courtesy of 5000 mgs of lysergic acid through this fourth-class delivery. We're the special people he's communicating with. We're in the cult. The back cover restates that the contents are *Strictly Personal*, that it's coming fourth class and it contains photographs.

The cover is a gatefold, and when you open it, there's a black-and-white photo of the band in shadow, wearing the weirdest sci-fi alien costumes. They'd been to Western Costume in Hollywood, where they rummaged through various outfits used in 1950s sci-fi films. The band photo on the inside cover shows – from left to right – Jeff Cotton, Alex St. Clair, John French and Jerry Handley, all in the weirdest outfits they could find, with Alex St. Clair in his 25th-century Quaker garb. They are setting out their credentials as a fully-fledged acid band – none weirder.

Interestingly, at the same shoot, photos were taken of them as their alter egos in their 25th-century Quaker robes. Those photos have never been used.

'Ah Feel Like Ahcid' (Van Vliet)

This track contradicts Don's later claim that he didn't use drugs. His use of marijuana and LSD has been well-documented by band members, friends and associates. Beefheart's assertion that the title was a corruption of 'I Feel Like I Said', does not hold much water with me.

The album is pure acid delta blues of the highest order from start to finish, starting with a distant tinkle of guitar, a persistent drum rhythm and the Captain singing solo in a lysergically-charged parody of Son House' 'Death Letter Blues'. LSD was often dispensed on stamps. Licking the stamps induced the trip. Don's poetry reflected the world opening up in colours, shapes and transformations, reds, blues and greens, his girl walking like on hard-boiled eggs, reality melting, like a church gospel meeting with that quacking, his girl sliding along, walking sexy, crazy, sleazy cheesy. Feels like heaven, like life is a movie. Somehow the words perfectly conjure up the world as seen through an acid trip. Sounds very Bermannish to me.

The sound at the beginning is a drumbeat based on a recording of Don's heartbeat – the actual heartbeat was used to end the track. It sets the tone. Following the a cappella section, the band slips in, with some harp and compelling blues riffs that augment the lyrics perfectly. They then fade out, leaving Don to sing solo, slapping his knee as accompaniment in an acid parody of Son House's 'Grinning In Your Face'. The track ends with Don yodelling that he ain't blue no more.

For some reason, Bob Krasnow broke the track into three: the beginning song, a section at the end of 'Trust Us' and a slight reprise at the end of the album. Some people don't like this. It works for me, but I'd also like to hear the three sections reunited.

'Safe As Milk' (Van Vliet)
It was bizarre that this track with the same name as the first album, was recorded subsequent to it. Had he already written it and not used it? Or did the album title inspire the later song?

The band comes in full-on, with the Captain a little back in the mix, then continues with vocals double-tracked. The sharp drumming propels the music along, with the guitars back in the mix and the vocals muffled. There's an extended drum solo coupled with a section of weird guitar noises drenched in phasing, reverb and panning, adding a full minute to the song.

This is the version that I heard first and came to know really well. I used to play this album to death, so I feel attached to it. Looking back and comparing this to take 5 on The *Mirror Man* Sessions, I can appreciate the differences. Take 5 was much cleaner, brighter and heavier. I don't mind the phasing and reverb here, but I prefer the crisper production of take 5.

'Trust Us' (Van Vliet)
By 1968, the zeitgeist had changed and this number was beginning to sound a little behind the curve, as it's a song of spirituality, searching, loving and trusting people. Things had moved on. Was the line 'Let the dying die' (I used to write that phrase on my exercise books at school!) a bible quote from Zachariah? The sentiment at the time was that the old did not get it at all – never trust anyone over 30.

This sounds muffled and muddy compared to the earlier sparkly versions from The *Mirror Man* Sessions. Bob has added spacey effects. There is also stereo panning and reverb on the voice. The end builds and jumps straight into the short second section of 'Ah Feel Like Ahcid'.

This is the track that I grew up listening to and love, but I find now that I prefer takes 6 and 9 from The *Mirror Man* Sessions. Take 6 has some fabulous drum rolls, but take 9 is the one that rocks my boat.

'Son Of Mirror Man – Mere Man' (Van Vliet)

The is a cut-down version of 'Mirror Man' from the *Mirror Man* album. It weighs in at just over five minutes in length, has alternative words, and has slightly different meaning for me. The lyric focus is on a duplicate world within that mirror.

It starts with a choppy rhythm guitar intro with underlying effects that lead into the body of the song. There are great vocals, duelling rhythm guitars and pounding bass that fill the track with energy and great impetus. The vocals and performance exude real power. There's a spacey little middle section with heavy drums, energetic bass, sound effects and cymbals, followed by a growly blues harp laden with distortion. The Captain's voice has also been altered and distorted. Don plays that weird oscillating harp right up to the end.

Don slagged this off, but to my ears, the production did not detrimentally affect the track. If anything, the weirdness adds to it. All sounds good to me.

'On Tomorrow' (Van Vliet)

A fabulous song in which the opaque poetry tells of an ideal world where we will all be brothers (and presumably sisters), love will create beauty, we will live how we want, with our hair growing wild, nature's wonders revealed, free from sorrow, grazing not killing, with our children possessing the golden wings with which to gain their freedom – a utopian dream that's a far cry from the capitalist nightmare being touted by the establishment.

The drums and bass dominate, setting up a persistent, complex rhythm. The first guitar lays down a repeating riff. The second guitar builds on that riff and weaves around it. Don announces that we're all brothers of tomorrow. The vocal is then double-tracked, with one track being heavily distorted to maintain interest. The two guitars chime together beautifully. They then riff together, interchanging complex rhythms. The song ends with a cacophony of bending notes.

'Beatle Bones N' Smokin Stones' (Van Vliet)

There's not a great deal to add about this version. It stands up well. There is a debate about whether this is a Rolling Stones/Beatles tribute or a mockery of them. I took it as a tribute. I reckon Don would've liked their spaced-out psychedelic period, even if he was often disparaging of some of their work, and he sure appreciated the R&B of the early-British Invasion to the point where he set about emulating those bands.

The song has a lot of acidic word association, and I think the phasing, distortion and effects, add to it, making it even stranger. I love the section where Don sings in harmony with the guitar. Perfect. Bob's production doesn't intrude for me, not on this one.

'Gimme Dat Harp Boy' (Van Vliet)

Bob's production was a minute and a half longer than the original, but not to the song's detriment. In this very punchy version, the Captain comes across as a psychedelicised Howlin' Wolf. There's some great blues harp, and the voice is distorted but without too many effects to obscure this bluesy track's brutal power. It's a very busy five minutes – guitars pushing the rhythm with clashing repeating refrains, thundering drums and pounding bass. The overriding riff is extremely potent with great energy. The track tails off into an elongated ending with background vocals, harp and discordant notes.

Liberty obvious thought it was the best track because they released it on their Gutbucket sampler. I suppose I do prefer the more-raw version on I May Be Hungry But I Sure Ain't Weird, but there's not much in it. The song is good enough to overcome all manner of different treatments.

'Kandy Korn' (Van Vliet)

On The *Mirror Man* Sessions, Bob Krasnow cut this down from eight minutes to five. Usually, that tightening makes a track sharper and more intense, but not in this case. 'Kandy Korn' has always been one of my favourites, and I immediately loved it when I first heard it on *Strictly Personal*. When I later heard the *Mirror Man* version, it became clear that the Krasnow's added effects layers had simply muffled the brilliance. That doesn't stop me liking the *Strictly Personal* version, but I think that of all the album's tracks, this one suffers the most. The *Mirror Man* version is sharp, raw and clear, with drums and bass to the fore, powering it along. On this version, they are subdued and hidden in the mix. For me, that's to the song's detriment.

Contrary to Don's assertions, I think he and Bob probably worked together on this album and got a little carried away with the latest psychedelic techniques. What they'd created was a great album that should've received far greater recognition, but in hindsight, they must've realised that – because of the song quality of the songs – the album could and should have been better produced: a lost opportunity for which Don made Bob the scapegoat.

Trout Mask Replica (1969)

Personnel:

Don Van Vliet; vocals, spoken word, tenor/soprano sax, bass clarinet, musette, simran horn, hunting horn, jingle bells

John 'Drumbo' French: drums, percussion, musical arrangements

Jeff 'Antennae Jimmy Semens' Cotton: guitar, slide guitar, lead vocals on 'Pena', 'The Blimp', 'Ella Guru'; Spoken voice on 'Old Fart At Play'

Bill 'Zoot Horn Rollo' Harkleroad: guitar, bottleneck guitar, flute on 'Hobo Chang Ba'

Mark 'Rockette Morton' Boston: bass, narration on 'Dachau Blues' and 'Fallin' Ditch'

Victor 'The Mascara Snake' Hayden: bass clarinet, backing vocals on 'Ella Guru', speaking voice on 'Pena'

Doug Moon: acoustic guitar on 'China Pig'

Gary 'Magic' Marker: bass on 'Moonlight On Vermont' and 'Veteran's Day Poppy'

Roy Estrada: bass guitar 'The Blimp'

Arthur Tripp III: drums, percussion on 'The Blimp'

Don Preston: piano on 'The Blimp'

Ian Underwood: alto sax on 'The Blimp'

Bunk Gardner: tenor sax on 'The Blimp'

Buzz Gardner: trumpet on 'The Blimp'

Frank Zappa: speaking voice on 'Pena' and 'The Blimp'

Richard 'Dick' Kunc: speaking voice on 'She's Too Much For My Mirror'

Producer: Frank Zappa, Don Van Vliet

Engineers: Don Van Vliet, Richard 'Dick' Kunc, Frank Zappa, John 'Drumbo' French

Studios: Sunset Sound Recorders, L.A.; Whitney Studios portable facilities, Glendale

Label: Straight

Album design: Cal Schenkel

Photography: Ed Caraeff, Cal Schenkel

The iconic *Trout Mask Replica* has influenced a multitude of artists, from The Beatles and Tom Waits to PJ Harvey and The Fall. The album's weirdness certainly pushed the boundaries of rock music. I was 20 when this album came out. I remember walking through Kingston upon Thames and seeing the cover in a High Street record shop window. I blinked and did a double-take because it wasn't due out for another month. Of course, I went in to check it out. The album turned out to be one from a bunch of records that the owner had brought back from the USA the week before. Unfortunately, one of the discs had been damaged in transit. It had a crack that went through two tracks, but it still played okay with just a slight click. Despite the damage, the guy wanted £5 for it, which – at the time, to me on a student grant – was a fortune. Nonetheless, I couldn't resist and I bought it.

Back home, I played it incessantly. The US pressing included a lyric sheet, and if memory serves me correctly, there were also a number of Beefheart doodles. I took that sheet into college with me to study and show my mates, but some reprobate stole it. This was extremely annoying because a number of lyrics were hard to decipher, plus it was a rather special and unique memento. I've never seen that lyric sheet anywhere else since, but to my delight, a friend recently found it on the web.

When the album was finally released in the UK, I was really miffed. The record company had made some kind of deal and it was on special offer for £3.20. Sadly, it didn't have a lyric sheet! However, I can confidently claim to be one of the first people in Britain to own this album. I heard it first! Possibly even before John Peel!! (Although, I bet they sent him an early pressing).

The story of *Trout Mask Replica* is so strange and complex that it really would make a good film. Oliver Stone ought to get on the case. To start with, there's Captain Beefheart's mental instability. John French said that one time when they were drunk together, Don confided in him that he'd been diagnosed with paranoid schizophrenia. If true, this might explain some of his bizarre and disturbing behaviour. With Don, it, was always difficult to determine what was real and what wasn't, what was simply his unique sense of humour, what was created as publicity hype, or what was actually a product of the reality in his head. What is certain is that his mind was unique, highly creative and gave rise to one of the greatest splurges of musical invention that we've ever heard. *Trout Mask Replica* is a monster of a work of art. The lifestyle, drug use and events of the period, all conspired to culminate in this masterpiece. I shall try to untangle them.

It all began with Don's falling out with Bob Krasnow over the production of *Strictly Personal*. Frank Zappa – Don's high-school friend and collaborator – was in the process of setting up two record labels: Straight and Bizarre. He offered Don the opportunity to record a double album with no restrictions and complete control over the production. Don leapt at it. The two men were extremely creative, inventive and extraordinary. Their collaborations sparked each other's creative juices. But they were also rivals – men with big egos and egocentricities, which meant both of them liked being in control. Sparks were bound to fly, and they did.

The next major component was the makeup of the band. Alex St. Clair and Jerry Handley had departed. Bill Harkleroad replaced Alex and was promptly renamed Zoot Horn Rollo. Two tracks were laid down with this lineup. Recorded at Hollywood's Sunset Sound Recorders seven months before the rest of the album, 'Veterans Day Poppy' and 'Moonlight On Vermont' featured Gary 'Magic' Marker temporarily filling in on bass. Shortly after, Mark Boston joined and was given the moniker Rockette Morton. He took over from Gary.

What I consider to be the Magic Band's greatest lineup was now established. All these guys had previously played together in blues bands (such as Blues In A Bottle) in the Lancaster area. They were seasoned blues musicians, eager and ambitious. They were years younger than Don and held him in awe. No doubt, Don saw them as talented and malleable. He set about dismantling their technique to make them play in a way that conformed to the unique style he envisioned. He moulded them by dominating the way they dressed, thought and behaved. The band became mere vehicles, conduits for his vision. The whole package – the music, performance, look and attitude, down to the way they held a cigarette – was a living art form to him. Artistic freedom unleashed a creative storm in Don's head that seemed to throw a switch. He had a concept for an album with no limits. He'd always been domineering, but now he became tyrannical. His music knew no boundaries. He drew on the blues, R&B, jazz, African, Native American, poetry and avant-garde, creating a fusion that was unprecedented in range, scope and vision.

In order to achieve the sounds he was imagining, Don made the musicians reinvent themselves. What followed was a seven-month regime that bordered on the insane. Zoot Horn Rollo talks of the Captain as more having the mentality of a sculptor than that of a musician. His idea was to use sound and people as tools. The band was forced to have a visual impact as well as a distinctive sound. He was aiming for the extreme avant-garde melded with jazz and blues. The songs were sound sculptures. Their polyphonic/polyrhythmic structures were repeating aural shapes. Sometimes one guitarist would be playing in 3/4 time while others played in 4/4, meeting up after 12 bars to start a new refrain. Zoot talked of how hard it was to do this, hanging on to the thrust of your own part against the thrust of everyone else's. What Don expected them to do was often musically impossible on guitar: playing nine simultaneous notes with the limitation of five fingers and six strings. Zoot talked of how they had to work out intricate means for delivering the sounds Don was requiring of them: methods that took hours and hours of practice.

The band was living in a small old house on Ensenada Drive, Woodland Hills, Los Angeles. They lived and breathed the music, with no time for anything else. Not that Don followed the tight regime he demanded of them – he kept himself mostly separate from the band, enjoying a far more relaxed lifestyle. He rarely rehearsed with them (telling them it was important that his vocals retain a spontaneous delivery and didn't become stale), emerging only to make demands or criticise their efforts. Life in the house became locked into a coercive bubble that rapidly took on all the negative attributes of a cult. He demanded that the band rehearse 14-18 hours a day. When they didn't do as he wanted (or sometimes simply randomly), Don would single one of them out for treatment. The unfortunate band member would be 'put in the barrel'. For hours they were berated and humiliated until they broke down. People visiting the house (as Ry Cooder did a few times) remarked on the menacing tension and atmosphere, calling it a 'Manson-esque cult'.

Was all this tight control and intimidation, part of Don's vision for melding the band into the unit he wanted? Or did it emanate from paranoia? It's possible that *Trout Mask Replica* sat already formed in Don's head. More likely, he had a basic idea and let it flow.

John French was the pivotal force. Don couldn't read or write music. John translated Don's ideas into reality. Most of the music was written on the piano, which was strange, as Don didn't play piano. He would dabble until he came up with the runs he wanted. John would write them down or select pieces from tapes Don had recorded, and then instruct the musicians on what to play. Sometimes Don would whistle or sing what he wanted John to transcribe. For seven months, the music, words and ideas flowed out of Don's uniquely-wired mind, and John interpreted them. Without John, we might not have this album.

Don immersed the band in the work of people like jazz saxophonist John Coltrane, composer Karlheinz Stockhausen, painter Salvador Dali and filmmaker Ingmar Bergman, which informed the musical vibe and attitude. He took the band to concerts, films and surrealist exhibitions as part of developing the unique style he was imposing on them. Don created an aura of aloofness and grandeur. He was the grandmaster, and the band were his fledglings. He commanded them, and the young musicians never questioned his authority. The lengthy and berating sessions – sometimes lasting 20 hours – were all part of his controlling mechanism. The band members became malleable tools, and he shaped them.

Zoot refutes the idea that Beefheart spent months writing the music. According to him, the Captain quickly bashed the runs out on the piano, adapting them until he was happy, and then let John French and the band work out the arrangements. Zoot observed that it was like painter Jackson Pollock trying to play bluesman John Lee Hooker: an image that sits in my head.

Frank had the idea of recording the album at the house as what he called 'an ethnic field record' – harking back to how Alan Lomax recorded the old blues musicians in the field. As it turned out, only one track was recorded this way (though portable recorders captured three other poetry tracks in Don's room). Tapes do exist of the band rehearsing in the house, and some of these have turned up on various albums. But Don was suspicious of Frank's idea because he thought Frank was trying to do it on the cheap. He demanded that the album be properly recorded in a studio. Frank acquiesced.

Don set about rehearsing the band until they were note-perfect. For seven months, they just slept and played. Life in the house became unbearable. There was little money coming in, just a few welfare cheques and help from friends and relatives. The band was actually starving for their art. For weeks they lived on only a handful of soya beans a day. They became so desperate that they went on a shoplifting spree at a local store. But they were caught stealing, and Frank had to bail them out as Don had no money.

By the time of the recording sessions, they'd been honed into a machine. They recorded all of the backing tracks for the entire album in one six-hour session: nearly all first takes. Don then spent the next few weeks adding the vocals and horns. The project was complete, but that was only the start of it. What followed next was the mythology. Through various interviews, an indication of the mayhem and weirdness started to emerge. The Captain claimed that none of the band had ever played an instrument, and he'd had to teach them from scratch. There may have been a slight grain of truth to this.

Obviously, all the band were highly competent musicians who had experience performing. What the Captain probably meant was that he had to retrain them to play in the way that he required in order to make the music he wanted.

Don claimed that the band didn't take drugs, an assertion the band members refuted – acid, speed and grass were ingredients in the melting pot that became the album. Then there was the strange matter of the tree surgeon. At the end of the recording, Frank received a bill from a tree surgeon. When questioned, Don explained that he'd been concerned about the loud music having a detrimental effect on the trees in the grounds of the house, and had called in a specialist. Frank shrugged, didn't want a fight with Don, and just paid.

A bone of contention with the band was that Don claimed to have written all the music and lyrics. This caused some aggravation with the band, who felt they'd greatly contributed: a matter that has never been adequately resolved.

The album cover is another masterpiece of surreal weirdness: Don wearing the hollowed-out head of a large fish (certainly not a trout). The back photo has the band looking hirsute, dressed in all manner of weird garb, with Antennae Jimmy Semens in a nightgown and Don brandishing a shadeless lamp. Inside the gatefold, a collage of separate band-member photos has been solarised into gaudy acid-drenched splashes of colour. They had an image to maintain! The visual was as important as the music.

Trout Mask Replica was not so much an album but more a collage of sound and visual sculpture. Every shred of music, appearance and behaviour had to be organised to fit the image, right down to the way they held a cigarette.

'Frownland' (Van Vliet)

The album starts with a complex song that many new initiates find difficult to access. I can see why. One has to persevere until its brilliance clicks into place. It's about a utopian dream; a better world that we can make for ourselves. Don preaches that we must get away from the nightmare we've created and escape into harmony with nature: the awe and wonder of the ocean and sky that we are part of. We have created a world of greed, violence and inequality that will end in doom. Don is offering a hand, leading us to a better way of living. Great positive sentiments.

Instantly you can feel the production's brightness, but that's when it starts to become difficult. Each guitar, bass and drum part has been carefully annotated, and each have their own rhythm and key. The opening lick is in 7/8. That gives it a real snap. The guitars then seem to go off on their own without regard for each other, while the complex drums and bass parts conspire to hold it all together. The polyrhythms – one in 5/4 and the other in 7/4 – make the piece sound jumbled as if a battle is going on. To the casual listener, this sounds chaotic, but it's not. The piece is carefully orchestrated, with each part appropriately arranged. Once your ears are tuned in, the music becomes wondrous and beautiful. The Captain is not producing bubble gum; this is of a different calibre and quality. His voice has strength and clarity as he sings this poem of optimism.

It's a powerful start, and, although it comes in at just under two minutes in length, the complexity makes it seem much longer. You instantly know that this album is going to be something extraordinary.

'The Dust Blows Forward 'N The Dust Blows Back' (Van Vliet)

This is a poem delivered in Don's inimitable style. The recitation is a performance packed with feeling, expression and joy. A happy, positive piece. It was recorded in the Woodland Hills house. The click is Don turning the tape recorder off and on. He and Frank liked the effect, so they left it in. The clicks make for an interesting irregular punctuation. When I first heard it I thought the clicks were the result of the crack in my vinyl album. I think those cracks contributed a few more clicks, but that only added to the effect.

The poem was written spontaneously, with Don repeatedly turning the tape recorder off in order to think of the next line. The lines follow one another like buses down the High Street. It hangs on the wordplay and rhyme that's coupled with the metre and rhythm. It's a poem about life and death, past ages, the serenity of nature and the pleasure to be found in a simple life in tune with the living world around us.

'Dachau Blues' (Van Vliet)

This is not as joyful; far from it. Having raised our mood with a vision of how wonderful life can be, Don brings us down to earth with a terrible image of how we humans are capable of turning life into a nightmare. The song uses the same shock value later deployed by Sex Pistols on 'Belsen Was A Gas' and Dead Kennedy's on 'Holiday In Cambodia'. Don summons up the horrors of Nazi concentration camps – Dachau was part of the Nazi 'final solution': one of the camps used in an attempt systematically eradicate the entire Jewish race: a genocide of epic proportions.

Don's voice booms in doom-laden mode, with the band striking up a melancholy set of riffs to a fast drum rhythm. The song changes pace as the vocal progresses. The overlaying of discordant horns emphasises the horror of the piece, adding a chilling tone of anguish and pain. Don berates the older generation, imploring them to not be warmongers. He deploys the spectre of the two world wars and begs the generation to change their ways before we end up with World War Three.

The piece segues into a short-spoken section: a recording of a visitor to the house relating a tale about rats.

'Ella Guru' (Van Vliet)

Who says Don couldn't do humour? This song is packed with it. That's Antennae Jimmy Semens playing the high voice of Ella, with The Mascara Snake doing the spoken interchange with Don. I think we've all known Ella Gurus. I can picture her now – a hippie girl decked out in a myriad of colours, breezing through life as high as a kite, conversing with the Moon.

The piece starts off in a slow dirge struck on interchanging guitar riffs. The drums in the centre hold it together. The pace picks up as Don's strong vocal holds a hilarious conversation with the flighty Ella. By the time we get to the chorus, it turns into a jaunty light number with breezy guitars interacting with percussion. It settles into a faster tempo with fabulous intertwining of guitar riffs and tempo changes. Don's short dialogue with the Mascara Snake is the first snippet of the 'Fast and Bulbous' poem, if it can be called a poem. It always makes me laugh (in a tapered kind of way).

'Hair Pie: Bake 1' (Van Vliet)

Straight into the avant-garde – a five-minute instrumental, the first minute and a half consisting of duelling saxophones in their unembellished fabulous discordant glory. Don was never taught to play the saxophone. Jeff Cotton claims to have given him one lesson. Don was very much into the experimental sounds of jazz saxophonists like Ornette Coleman. His influence can be detected here. As with the piano, Don just experimented until he produced the noises he wanted. Some people hate it: I think it's perfect – Ornette Coleman on acid, creating demented phrases over the top of agonised wails.

After that opening section, the band comes in, the drums become dominant and heavier guitars break through. Sparring horns persist over the top, creating that free-form jazz feel. There's a punchy section with chiming guitars playing in synch and changing polyrhythms, before the horns finally drop out.

The title is another example of Don's humour – hair pie being urban slang for oral sex. The talking section at the end was recorded in the house. Two young people had moved into the area and dropped 'round to check out what the noise was all about. Don has great pleasure playing them this latest offering. Given the sexual connotation, he aptly calls it a bush recording.

'Moonlight On Vermont' (Van Vliet)

This was recorded seven months earlier at Hollywood's Sunset Sound and has Gary 'Magic' Marker on bass; Rockette had not yet joined the band. The drum and cymbal intro unleashes a supernova of power as the band launches into an unceasing assault on our cerebral cortexes, starting with two guitars trading riffs – one leading, one answering – as the bass walks along in the background. The Captain's amazing voice is belting out lines full of power and expression. Traded guitar phrases are scintillating over a seminal thumping rhythm.

Nobody had a voice like Don's. Here he takes Chester Burnett (Howlin' Wolf') to another level. The song is more accessible than many of the album's other tracks and is relentless in its clout. Two-thirds of the way through, a sustained guitar note heralds the band breaking into a searing parody of 'Old-Time Religion': a traditional Afro-American spiritual first noted in 1872. This raunchy, hard-core, demonic gospel is like no religion I've heard of – it's more like space-age spirituality. Beefheart roars into another dimension.

The phrase 'Come out t' show dem' is taken from a 1966 Steve Reich piece called 'Come Out'. The poem describes the effects of the lysergic moon on our sanity. The lyric takes us on a surreal moonlit journey where nothing is normal. 'Everybody's gone high society' is the play-on-words. We're in a world where peeing-boy statues come to life, elephants eat peanuts on Main Street, and all the animals escape from the zoo. The moonlight (or acid) releases everyone from the mundane. 'Hope lost his head'. It's a poem of two halves, just like the music. This new space-age religion has no room for affliction or restriction but can work for all of us. The repeating lines reinforce the message's power: that this old-time religion is a new force that can release us all!!

'Pachuco Cadaver' (Van Vliet)

I'm not really sure why this title (Mexican gangster's corpse) was chosen. The poem appears to be about a flamboyant Mexican lady who dresses to kill, has a vivid past life, and still does at the age of 99. Although pachucos are mentioned, there are no corpses. Perhaps the señora is a metaphor. Perhaps she is the matriarch of a Chicano gang. The poem describes her as a vibrant character who dominates the room with her dress, her eyes and her manner. According to other accounts, the poem is about an old and colourful Mexican car in a parade. She's a delight.

The spoken intro is another snatch of the poem 'Fast And Bulbous'. It leads into an appealing drums/bass-driven song with rhythm guitars laying down their intricate interchanges. Seemingly oblivious to each other, they do their own thing in different textures yet gel together. Everything is carefully synchronised. As the music changes, the vocal begins: almost recited instead of sung. The rich, resonant voice embellishes the poem. The music is busy but not intrusive. The tempo picks up, slows down and picks up again. The complex drumming anchors the piece. Towards the end, we get Don's saxophone-playing (almost melodic for a change) in a repeating refrain; discordant yet melodic.

Somebody thought this track was accessible and catchy enough to release as a single. But it was never going to be hit-parade material. Being far from simple, it requires intense listening.

'Bills Corpse' (Van Vliet)

This title 'Bill's Corpse' perhaps came either from the state of Bill Harkleroad when he arrived from an acid cult (wasted like a skeleton), or Bill the goldfish, that died and was ceremoniously buried in the garden.

The poem is rather obscure. I've always interpreted it as being a metaphor for the way we've treated the planet. The words are extremely vivid and moving - the ash and bloated fish, the crying children, skeletons, death and destruction. 'She' can 'look at us with love and let us fall, or have us all'.

The band starts with a steady underlying rhythm and intermeshing guitars. At first, it's as if each musician is playing a different song. But as your ear tunes in, you can hear how it all interacts. The poem is sung/recited over the top. At the end, the band plays quietly to emphasise the words, and the final line is sung without backing. It has been said that Don failed to get the timing of the words right, so consequently, the track ends before he finishes. Either way, the result is effective.

'Sweet Sweet Bulbs' (Van Vliet)

Another vision of paradise that we could make on Earth if we gave up our greedy, violent ways. Don invites us into the garden of nature to relax, bask in the wonders and refresh ourselves. It's a place where his lady has found herself as Queen on a throne. He wants us to come and live freely in the midst of this beauty.

The bass – high in the mix and more pronounced than usual – leads with the drums. The song progresses through sound and tempo changes, always returning to the basic central riff, creating a beautiful complexity. The drumming's constant foundation metamorphoses so the instrumental refrains can coalesce around it.

'Neon Meate Dream Of A Octofish' (Van Vliet)

If these really are the meate dreams of an octofish, I don't think I'd really enjoy meeting one. It's a nonsense poem, forming visual images and squirming visions. It's a fantastic vision of a mythical, prehistoric sea beast, which sounds like the Captain was spouting a stream of word association and allowing it to flow. Very 'fast and bulbous', with maybe a small amount of tapering.

The poem is recited over the complex rhythms of two guitars. The noise in the background is like the sound of a whale dreaming. The drums and bass set up a constant rhythm, leading the guitars through many different time signatures. At the poem's completion, the sounds become louder, with horn-wailing in the foreground, building into a cacophony of whale noises. I think the octofish are mating.

It always reminds me of The Doors' 'Horse Latitudes', though that is probably a sacrilege.

'China Pig' (Van Vliet)

The house might've had a scary regime, but people still dropped by to visit. One of these was Doug Moon: a former stalwart of the band, and an excellent blues musician.

'China Pig' was recorded at the house on a portable tape recorder during an impromptu session. Doug set up a blues guitar riff in A, reminiscent of John Lee Hooker, and Don sang along to it. Except for the words, it sounds like a standard blues, and is performed brilliantly by two consummate blues artists. The lyric propels the song into a different world. Don's breath can be heard. I'm not sure if that's an intentional effect, but it works well. The yodelling at the end is signature Beefheart. Those years of playing in the early band enabled them to spontaneously gel, producing a brilliant performance.

Has ever an adult song been written about a piggy bank? Not until Don wrote this. In life, money is needed to buy food and clothing, and Don recounts how he raided his piggy bank in desperation. Don describes how he killed his china pig – 'I got him by the snout, 'N I takes him by the cuff, 'N I whipped out m' fork, 'N I poked at um.' He suggests that he used the money to feed his neighbours. 'I remember my china pig. I fed the neighbourhood. It was uh big neighbourhood. Uh lot uh people liked my pig.' Perhaps a bit fanciful. There is no record of Don's early philanthropic ventures though he did drive his father's bread van and may have helped out by dropping off some supplies to needy friends.

'My Human Gets Me Blues' (Van Vliet)
This was principally directed at John 'Drumbo' French, who was a Christian: something that Don found difficult to come to terms with. Around the time of this recording – during one of their 'in the barrel' sessions – he orchestrated an actual physical attack on John.

The song is Don's attack on religion. He focuses on the guilt trip imposed on a young trans person because of their sexuality. He cites the Christian idea of a judgemental God in the sky and the fear of eternity in Hell. He states that Jesus is never coming back, and mockingly describes the prospect of a heaven where you can be young and wear your favourite dress and even bring your dog and hog. It'll be just dandy. A myth created by humans is enough to give you the blues.

The number starts with drums and a simple bass motif emphasising the slow rhythm. Two guitars with very different tones set off on their own refrains: one chiming, the other more subdued. They set up a swinging rhythm, exchanging lead and rhythm roles, deploying varying phrases that separate and reunite. With immaculate patterns and bursts of lead guitar, the number speeds up and slows down. There follows a quiet section – just Don's voice with the right-side slide guitar – then it's back to the shuffle and a faster section. Exhilarating stuff. Don's voice is fabulous: resonant, powerful and expressive.

'Dali's Car' (Instrumental) (Van Vliet)
This was the first number composed for the album. It's an abstract instrumental that Don described as 'a study in dissonance', inspired by a visit he and the band made to a Salvador Dali installation called Rainy Taxi. Unusually there are no drums or percussion. Starting with a slow strummed electric guitar, another guitar enters in a higher register and the two play in tandem: a duet between Zoot and Antennae Jimmy Semens. The bass comes in with a few notes, and the guitar pattern follows.

'Hair Pie: Bake 2' (Instrumental) (Van Vliet)

Unlike the previous instrumental, this does have drums (John French put cardboard on his drums to get the desired deadening effect), and sets off at a rollicking pace. A second dose of oral sex is on the cards.

Beefheart had been listening to composers such as Stravinsky and Stockhausen, and some of their style has rubbed off in the creation of this bitonal number. There's a dominating guitar riff on the left side, with support coming from a second one on the right. The bass positively bubbles with beautiful runs. I love the section where the two guitars harmonise the refrain. Everything is so perfectly synchronised. The immaculate drums lead and change the tempo as one guitar dominates, then the other, with the bass setting brilliant patterns throughout: never monotonous. The invention is maintained until the end when the sleigh bells shoot off into infinity.

'Pena' (Van Vliet)

This begins with a third section of 'Fast And Bulbous': an interchange between the Captain and the Mascara Snake (Victor Hayden). They recorded this verbal opening on the house's trusty tape recorder. They attempt it twice, getting the humorous words wrong and breaking down in laughter before finally getting it right. This leads into the instrumental number.

It starts with a sedate rhythm and leisurely guitar riffs. The same can't be said for the rest of the number. Amidst a cacophony of manic background noises, Antennae Jimmy Semens (aka Jeff Cotton) belts out the main vocal – a great splurge of words – in a high-pitched surreal voice. The madness continues in the background, but the band somehow maintain a degree of sanity.

Now we must turn to the poem which blows the mind most elegantly. Pena sits on a waffle iron with smoke billowing from between her legs. She's hot! Quite an image. The observer watches, vomits and views her from a thousand facets. Who is this? A fly, perhaps? An alien with multifaceted eyes? Who knows? Is this a dream? Sometimes it's hard to understand the essence of reality contained in acid, and this is surely an example of an acid vision. Are these just nonsense words? They're certainly very sexual in a heavily metaphorical manner. Perhaps they are beyond the scope of understanding. Maybe that's the intention.

'Well' (Van Vliet)

This is reminiscent of a field blues holler. Sounding rather like Paul Robeson, Don's rich and expressive voice recites in a great rhythm, without a shred of backing. Some might say without a shred of sense too, but I think there is abstract meaning there, which settles into the brain's cortex, subliminally delivering the content. The words are not just surreal, they are Dadaist with individual lines creating visual images: 'Mind cracked like custard', 'Feathers of solid chrome'. I think this song is about a really cruel world. Don uses the words of a resolute person who is stoically defiant, fighting against the harshness of existence. Or maybe that's just my understanding. I think this is one of his poems that means different things to different people.

'When Big Joan Sets Up' (Van Vliet)

A rare song to be written about body image. Big Joan worries because her hands are too small, and not that her body is too big. I love the way the emphasis is on the hands and not her obese body. The song contains humour but is also a sad reflection on our obsession with the perfect body. But I find it hard to picture the Captain showing such kindness and understanding. I wonder whether Big Joan is a metaphor for something else: some people have suggested the Moon.

The band starts in the familiar pattern of two guitars trading riffs: John and Mark providing a steady base to work from. The Captain – having forgotten his harmonica – comes in with some scat singing. The music comes to a halt for the horn section, which – though it sounds like two half-strangled brontosauri having a fight – fits in perfectly. The band returns. It feels like the guitarists have shut everything out and are concentrating on their own rhythmic parts without regard to anything else. They're in a world of their own. The horns are in the background. The bass is sublime.

So much is going on in this mix, it becomes hectic: a psychotic jazz blues on benzedrine. Much is buried. It would be interesting to dig into the music, isolate and unearth some of the incredible refrains being played in there. The piece is chaotic but has a great melody that carries it through. It's meaningless but full of insight, so frenzied that it shouldn't work, yet it does. It hangs together. That's what's so great about Beefheart's music – it pulls you in; the music is complex; the lyrics seem full of meaning, but everything is just beyond one's grasp. You find yourself hooked. It propels you. It's visceral. It tugs at the cortex. Rewarding.

There is a false stop – silence punctuated by a few honks from what sounds like tortured geese. The music starts up again with the rhythm guitars setting a steady refrain that holds everything together, while Don does his best Howlin' Wolf impression: quoting from the Wolf's '300 lbs Of Joy'. The horn finale is anguished: the Captain sounding as if trying to strangle an octofish. Phew – a work of genius. A museum piece.

'Fallin' Ditch' (Van Vliet)

A song about depression and death to cheer us up. Don is determined that life won't bring him down. The sun will come out. That 'fallin' ditch ain't going to get my bones'. The spoken-word intro – back-and-forth with Rockette Morton – is hilarious. The guitars trade riffs over the backing's slow dirge, but the bass is prominent and I can see why it's high in the mix – it's divine: a fluid, bubbling, joyous sound! The impressive vocal is resolute. The tempo picks up, the bass burbles and the guitars meld. The mood changes to one of determination and optimism.

'Sugar 'N Spikes' (Van Vliet)

Hours could be spent picking away at this poem's surreal imagery. If it were intended to make perfect sense, it probably failed. There are some spectacular lines: 'Pies steam stale shoes move broom 'n pale', ''N walks 'n lights 'n chains coughin' smoke whoopin' hope'. Don sure liked playing with words, rhyme, alliteration and sound. The meaning might be elusive, but the gist is clear: he's in love and has a snazzy little lady. The wordplay Don brings to bear on the children's poem 'sugar and spice and all things nice' is fun. The two of them are off to see 'the navy blue vicar'.

It's an antidote to the previous track: bouncy, energetic and full of vim. The short electric guitar intro leads straight into the band going at it full tilt, and the Captain right on top of his game, belting out the vocals impeccably. The piece's structure is superb – the way it changes rhythm and tempo, and builds for the choruses, though much more orthodox than usual. It gets you rocking – infectious enough to have been a mainstream hit despite being inherently Beefheart-esque. That last section is as good as music gets.

'Ant Man Bee' (Van Vliet)

The imagery of different colour ants fighting over a sugar cube is a powerful metaphor for the stupidity of mankind with its racism, greed and belligerence. In contrast, Don uses the analogy of the bee and its relationship with the flower for how we should live in harmony with nature. He was certainly an idealist, a humanitarian environmentalist and visionary. For once, the lyrics are not obscured in surreal mists. The word 'uhuru' is repeated, and means 'freedom' in Swahili.

The music is interesting, compelling and extraordinary in a Beefheartian way. John French said, 'Don's drum ideas were sometimes amazing. 'Ant Man Bee' for example, has one of the cleverest beats I've heard in my life'. It's mind-boggling that Don was able to conceive every note and orientate the instruments and poem in such a way that this complex arrangement makes sense, particularly as he couldn't read or write music. It was all in his head, out of his head.

All the ingredients we've come to expect are deployed. The guitar on the left is bright and cheery; the one on the right more subdued. The drum rhythms lead the number and are extremely complicated. The bass gets into a hypnotic groove. Don's voice booms, so full of expression rising, testing his fabulous range. The poem knits with the music, reflecting the tempo changes.

We have a song of two parts. The first is centred on the poem; the second, longer section more of a free-jazz fusion with Coltrane-esque wails of sax like a hippo in pain, then in agony. It's surprising when he hits a melodic part! But it works. The contrast between the atonal and the melodic creates tension. Fab.

'Orange Claw Hammer' (Van Vliet)

This is sung a cappella in a heartrending interpretation of the poetry. It tells the story of a man – a husband and father – who was enticed away to sea, shanghaied and taken to a distant land, where he raised seven children with a beautiful dark-skinned girl. 30 years later, he returns as a peg-legged hobo in rags, looking for work as a roundhouse man. He finds a child who he thinks is his daughter, and recounts to her something of his life and travels. He is deluded. After 30 years away, that little girl is far more likely to be his granddaughter. This synopsis hardly does justice to the colourful imagery and amazing word deployment. 'And an oriole sang like an orange/His breast full o' worms, and his tail clawed the evenin' like a hammer'. Don's delivery – stuttering in places and wracked with emotion – brings the poem to life, drenched in pathos, regret and anguish.

'Wild Life' (Van Vliet)

This is about freedom. Living within society is compromising, even claustrophobic. Societies put pressure on people to conform. Don was not the conforming type. He saw conformity as a limitation that crushed the life out of people. This pressure had affected his parents and family, and he wasn't about to let that happen to him. He valued his wild life; his freedom.

The poem has an element of humour and play-on-words. Don was planning to head up a mountain to live free in nature and persuade some wild life in the form of bears to take him in. That forms a mad picture in my head – him sitting around in a cave with a bunch of bears feasting on berries!

The music is slow with evolving riffs and polyrhythms. Don sings in quite a low register, with theatrical elements: 'Before they take my wife!' The sax is some of the most fluid I've heard him play. There are sections that are pure free-form jazz. The vocal and sax call-and-response works well.

Don always had a love of nature. 'Wild life is a man's best friend' can be taken in two ways.

'She's Too Much For My Mirror' (Van Vliet)

The last comment, 'Oh shit, I don't know how I'm gonna get that in there', is telling. It sums up how the songs were constructed. These tracks were recorded after the band rehearsed themselves to death, usually in one take. Don would later record the vocal and embellish with sax. On this occasion, he's not managed to fit the full vocal onto the track. That's not surprising, because he never used headphones while recording his vocal – just relying on the minimal sound leaking into the booth from the studio. The amazing thing is that he usually managed to match everything up so well.

This time the words overrun the music. It's a wordy song but works perfectly well as it is. The lines outside the music seem to add emphasis.

The intro was courtesy of sound engineer Dick Kunc. The poem relates a guy's love for a beautiful girl who spends time preening herself. She was 'too much for my mirror' – too beautiful: a past love from back on the farm with the butterflies and corn. He followed her to the bitter cold of Chicago, only to find she didn't love him after all: 'She was just a floozy'. His mother had warned him to be choosy, but he'd ignored her. Now he can't get over the girl and cannot even bear to look at himself in that mirror. The lyric is probably a metaphor for the beauty of harmony with nature, as opposed to a harsher life in the frigid city.

'Hobo Chang Ba' (Van Vliet)
A hobo rides the blinds, waking up – feeling the vibration of the wagon's wooden floor as the train rolls along – thawing out from the cold of the night, looking for hope in the new day. The hobo is the epitome of freedom: not necessarily always pleasant.

Don adopts a deep theatrical voice for this track, which John French described as a 'voice reminiscent of the African singer on John Coltrane's 'Kulu Se Mama''. Twiddling guitar and thudding drums settle into the freight train rhythms. Beautiful drums, bass and guitar exchanges give the track bite.

'The Blimp' (Mousetrapreplica) (Van Vliet)
'This is recorded through a fly's ear' – an old-style telephone – straight from the Captain's house into the studio. Frank Zappa taped the call and put it on a backing track he'd recorded with his own band. That's Jeff 'Antennae Jimmy Semens' Cotton excitedly reciting the poem, and the Mothers Of Invention playing the music. This was obviously the one that was going to make them all famous.

The poetry sizzles with searing wordplay, nonsense, alien imagery, rhyme and rhythm. What are these drazy hoops?? What is this blimp? Is there something sexual about it? An alien mothership from outer space? A dirigible? Breasts? Who knows! 'The tape's a trip': go with it! It'll get you outta the gutter!

This track is crazy, becoming more and more manic as it progresses. The Mothers Of Invention set up a really tight repeating refrain that suddenly stops, then, after a long pause, starts again. There's a weird section of wailing sax which sounds like a whale giving birth. The vocal is breathlessly recited over the top! Somehow it works. It's 'The Blimp'. There's nothing else quite like it! Music from an alien culture.

'Steal Softly Through Snow' (Van Vliet)
Don wants to leave this world for somewhere better on the other side of that mirror. This world is too nasty. We humans are so destructive; we are destroying nature, building our roads over the beauty, messing up the countryside. We're back to the philosophy of the Native Americans, who endeavoured to live without leaving their mark on the landscape.

A great shuffling intro from guitar and drums settles into a repeating refrain. Total precision from two guitars with changing keys involves the mixing of tonal and atonal, each guitar with a distinct tone. The drums and bass are in perfect alignment. Over the top of this body of sound, the song is sheer musical genius. There are many changes, but towards the end, the song lurches forward into a faster tempo, with Don struggling to spout the words in a manic frenzy. So complex. So varied. So together. The message is completely clear: 'Man lives a million years, and still, he kills'.

'Old Fart at Play' (Van Vliet)
Chunky guitar and strong bass, gel with the drums. Don recites the poem. The music drops out towards the end, exposing his expressive delivery, which ascends into a delirious dreamy state for the last two lines. That's Jeff Cotton remarking how heavy the poem is. I'm not sure it is that heavy. It's a surreal tale from down on the farm, with an old guy playing a prank, donning a wooden trout mask to scare the shit out of his wife, who is baking in the kitchen. Far from being scared, she seems to take it in her stride. I guess she's used to him. She opens the window to let out the kitchen smells. He closes the mask air holes, and breathes in from a perfume bottle atomiser: all ultra-weird but not exactly heavy; just kinda fun.

'Veteran's Day Poppy' (Van Vliet)
One of the best anti-war songs ever written. The poem is from the viewpoint of a mother who is lamenting the loss of her son: a soldier who returned home seriously messed up from his experiences in Vietnam. The symbolism is of poppies and 'high': alluding to heroin.

This is the other song recorded at Hollywood Sunset Sound Recorders studios in August 1968, seven months before the others, featuring Gary 'Magic' Marker on bass. Frank Zappa showed rookie Bill Harkleroad (Zoot Horn Rollo) the chords. A fabulous intro stumbles to a halt, the guitar sets the rhythm and the voice crashes in. The backing is almost buoyant in contrast to the sentiment. The lead licks are tasty, the drum patterns immaculate. We transition to the second half, where the musicianship continues to shine and the guitars are perfectly synchronised, mirroring each other superbly in their different tones. There's even a minor-9 chord in there!

What's quite clear is that in the 52 years since the album's release, it has been rare for any other band to have matched the sheer scope, musicianship, invention and complexity of this revolutionary avant-garde jazz rock band. They were and are on a different planet. Sheer crazy genius.

Contemporary Recordings
'Willie The Pimp' (Zappa) From Hot Rats by Frank Zappa (1969)
Frank Zappa was producing his second solo album at the same time Don was working on *Trout Mask Replica*. Hot Rats was mainly jazz fusion instrumentals, but Zappa drafted Don in for the 'Willie The Pimp' vocal. The pair had been friends and collaborators since being at Antelope Valley High School back in Lancaster. Their relationship was one of respect and closeness, but also intense rivalry. It came as a shock to members of the Magic Band – who were in awe of the older Don and had suffered under his tyrannical rule – to see

the way Frank behaved with Don. It was like the two were still High School chums. Frank called him Donny. Occasionally Don would take one of the band members to Frank's house, where they'd spend the entire night drinking, talking and listening to music. At Frank's place, the Captain Beefheart persona disappeared. They were seeing a different person.

By this time, Frank was very successful. He could afford to rent a decent house and employ people. Much to his chagrin, Don was still living on the breadline. Frank would often pop around to Don's with beer or food parcels, which must've been humiliating.

Although his second solo outing, this album was the first that Frank was recording without the Mothers Of Invention. When he needed a good vocalist, he naturally turned to Don.

This starts with a fabulous compulsive repeating violin and guitar riff with drums and bass laying down the spine. Don appears larger than life: a flashy pimp in khaki trousers and shiny shoes; hair greased back. Full of bravado, he projects this image, his voice booming.

The words tell the story of Willie before slipping into a wordplay sequence: 'Hot meat, Hot rats, Hot zits, Hot wrists, Hot ritz, Hot roots, Hot Soots'. The mention of 'Soots' is interesting. Soots was the name of a band they both played in back in Lancaster. After Don finishes his tale, he does some whoopin' and wailin'. As Frank's guitar comes in, the riff breaks up and they settle into a long free-form section. The violin riff returns as the track comes to an end.

Lick My Decals Off, Baby (1970)

Personnel:
Don Van Vliet: vocals, bass clarinet, tenor sax, soprano sax, harmonica
Bill 'Zoot Horn Rollo' Hackleroad: guitar and bottleneck guitar, arrangement
Mark 'Rockette Morton' Boston: bass
John 'Drumbo' French: drums, percussion
Art 'Ed Marimba' Tripp: percussion
Producer: Don Van Vliet
Recorded at the Record Plant, West Hollywood
Label: Straight/Reprise
Album concept: Peacock ink
Don Van Vliet: back cover painting
Ed Thrasher: photography and art direction

After the extraordinary *Trout Mask Replica*, I didn't know what to expect. I was hoping for more of the same, but I didn't believe anyone could maintain that level of creativity, particularly now that the fabulous Jeff Cotton (the intrepid Antennae Jimmy Semens) was no longer involved. How were they going to achieve that telepathic, ground-breaking dual guitar attack? With some trepidation, I bought *Lick My Decals Off, Baby* on the day of release. I wasn't in the habit of buying new albums because I was still a penniless student. I usually haunted the secondhand record shops searching out bargains. I made exceptions for Roy Harper and Captain Beefheart. I was not disappointed.

The album picks up where *Trout Mask Replica* left off. This time the song refrains are longer and feel more developed. They retain their complex structures, polyrhythms, intricate bass runs and poetic lyrics, but Don sounds happier, with his sense of humour coming through. *Trout Mask Replica* seems experimental, fragmentary, with a range of ideas and innovations; on Lick My Decals Off, Baby, those ideas have coalesced and become coherent and focussed; the ideas developed, creating a unified body of work. Maybe this change was the result of them no longer living communally. I'm not sure, but I like it even better!

The album title is reflected in the cover. A decal is a stick-on label. Don said he wanted to throw away all labels (But I reckon it was just sexual: Lick them decals off, baby). The music and band stood on its merits, not its image. Hence the front cover shows them incongruously dressed in tuxedos and bow ties at a stately home (actually a film set). The back cover features a painting and poem. The painting is quite abstract, but to me suggests a colourful bug with two long legs smoking a long spliff. The poem is like another version of 'Lick My Decals Off, Baby'.

The album was made in a similar fashion to *Trout Mask Replica*. Unfortunately, following that recording, Don dismissed John French from the band (It seems they had a violent altercation terminating in Don throwing him down the stairs). With no music arranger, it now fell to Zoot to take over the role. He listened to all Don's recordings, and taught the other musicians in a similar way to John French: not an enviable task. John later made up with Don, rejoining the band just prior to recording the album, but by then, all the arrangements were complete.

The Captain was ahead of the game when it came to promoting the album. MTV would've been proud. The band made a video of the title track and filmed a bizarre television commercial. Though a very straight commentary introduced the band, the minute-long Dada-esque commercial featured snippets from 'Woe-Is-Uh-Me Bop' as a hand flicked cards, Beefheart stood in weird pose, and the masked band shuffled across the screen playing kitchen utensils! The video terminated with a large bowl of white gunk kicked over on to the white line of a road. The video was hilarious and totally surreal, but I'm not sure it gained any converts.

Enigma Retro released the album on CD in 1989. Rhino Records released in 2014 as part of the four-disc box set Sun Zoom Spark: 1970 To 1972, which included Lick My Decals Off, Baby, *The Spotlight Kid*, *Clear Spot* plus outtakes. Rhino again reissued Lick My Decals Off, Baby in 2015, with no bonus tracks.

'Lick My Decals Off, Baby' (Van Vliet)

Even though Beefheart said that licking decals off meant to remove all labels (which just might work for the title and cover photo), that explanation doesn't cut it with this song. This is about sex; pure animal sex, nothing more. He wants to lick you everywhere it's pink and wants you to lick his decals off. We've gone way past squeezing lemons here. He doesn't want to hold your hand, he wants to swallow you whole! The man's a wild beast! 'She stuck out her tongue and the fun begun'. The inference is that sex went wrong when religion made it a sin: taking us away from being animals in harmony with nature.

The guitar and bass entwine in synchrony like mating serpents, and the drums gallop along as if the cavalry's coming. Then suddenly, everything transitions to a slow tempo as the Captain appears, voice anguished, slurring and sleazy. He wants the whole 'kitchen sink'. The music speeds up for a brief frenzy before returning to the languid lasciviousness. The Captain is leering and sexy: 'Heaven's sexy as hell'. Then we're belting along again. The drums sound like flailing bongos, and the repeating guitar riff hits your gut. 'It's all about the birds 'n' the bees 'n' where it all went wrong'.

'Doctor Dark' (Van Vliet)

Still on the theme of sexuality, here comes Doctor Dark in what feels like a Victorian horror film. Whatever this mysterious figure is dispensing, the little girl has put aside her toys. The black leather woman has a new white, white child.

The band pounds along like the coach clattering down the cobbled road with horses' hooves kicking up sparks. Don's vocals cut through the music like a foghorn. His delivery is interspersed with bursts of drums and Mark Boston taking the incessant bass line into another dimension. The guitar spits out complex runs as the music thunders along in this sinister setting, the opaque lyrics smacking of lasciviousness.

'I Love You, You Big Dummy' (Van Vliet)
The band had a whale of a time recording this track, and at times it sounds as if a whale was involved!. You can hear their joy and laughter. It's funky. The bass sets up a groovy rhythm. All around, there's unleashed madness – the Captain yodelling at the top of his register, saxophones squealing and harmonica playing. The vocal declaring 'I love you, you big dummy' is repeated like a mantra. The poem plays with words: 'No body has love'; 'Love has no body'. I don't think I've ever heard Don laughing like this, relaxed and enjoying himself. So, 'Breathe deep, breathe high, breathe life, I don't breathe a lie' – dig it, it's fun – 'Quit asking why'.

'Peon' (Van Vliet)
Bill Harkleroad's guitar-playing is immaculate as he stridently works his way through this beautiful instrumental, fully augmented by Mark on bass. The two – playing together in complex harmony – seem psychically attached like two strands of DNA. The fabulous melody screws itself into your brain with attack and bite. The later Harkleroad version on the Mallard album has a different feel altogether: smoother, slower, wistful and mellow. I love both versions.

This piece was written in praise of Don's wife Jan, though it should really be 'Paean' (a poetic term for praise) or 'Paeon' (a hymn of thanksgiving) rather than Peon (a low-skilled labourer). Perhaps Don had just had a fight with Jan, he was playing around with words or just couldn't spell.

As with all of Don's songs, there's conjecture as to how much is his work and how much came from the other musicians. On this album, Don worked out all the guitar and bass pieces on the piano. Zoot was the conduit. Sometimes Don would sing, hum or whistle the part. When it came to making the pieces work, there were obviously parts that had to be adapted: sometimes radically. Just how much adaptation was necessary varied between songs. There's a very strong case for the other musicians being credited in order to receive the recognition they deserve – Zoot and Drumbo in particular, and certainly Rockette on this track.

'Bellerin' Plain' (Van Vliet)
The freight train is 'bellerin'' across the plain; the band chugging along, labouring up the incline, past the willow's gnarled roots. No jokers or fakers on board. It's carrying that sugar beet as it rolls down the track. The tempo increases. The misty obscurity of the words on paper, comes to life when the music enflames them. Don's singing narration invigorates their meaning. The bass solo showcases Mark Boston's importance and the versatility he brought to the band.

'Sunnyland' is a reference to Elmore James. Elmore, a Chicago blues singer, specialising in amazing electric slide guitar, recorded a track called Sunnyland in 1954. The track was about a train that is taking his girl away from him.

Drums and bass play with each other, marimba and guitar creating a different quality to anything that's gone before – first complementing each other, then moving into perfect synchronicity. The band thunders back in as the freight picks up speed, rolling faster along that track. All aboard. The sax wails like a full-blown train whistle, it's bellowing, fit to raise the dead. I still don't know what parapliers are! But that doesn't matter. This is one of the greatest railroad songs ever.

'Woe-Is-Uh-Me-Bop' (Van Vliet)
In this song, the Captain laments the sorry state of the world and the mess we humans are making of it. 'Woe-Is-Uh-Me-Bop. Please don't let them ruin it'.

The repeating groove expresses the cycle of anguish, with warm overtones. Listen to that marimba blend in with the guitars, bass and drums. Unique! The Captain's voice is full of despair and misery. When the music drops out, he's left alone with sparse marimba notes. You can clearly hear his sorrow.

'Japan In A Dishpan' (Instrumental) (Van Vliet)
Not the usual Beefheart instrumental. This track is a vehicle for his sax-playing, starting with melodic wailing before the band brings a bedrock of solidity with exquisite drumming, beefy guitar riffs and a wandering bass going over, under and around. It's brutal, industrial, and sounds a lot like Yoko Ono. As it progresses, the sax becomes more discordant, complex and tortured, with its repeating phrases squiggling all over the backing. This is maths rock, following set patterns and intervals. It takes a few listens to get into, but once your ear is acclimatised, the effort is worthwhile.

'I Wanna Find A Woman That'll Hold My Big Toe Till I Have To Go' (Van Vliet)
The starts with a funky backing of bass and marimba working in unison. The first guitar plays in a deep register, with the second finishing off each riff higher. As the vocal begins, the backing changes.

To play around with the words, not only does Don want to find a woman who will hold his big toe, he wants to play with those yams all night long. He wants to find a swirly blue plastic ocarina, five miles long. Those sweet potatoes have dirty brown hair. He wants everything to go on until he has to sow his last sweet potato. I can't help thinking there are sexual metaphors lurking in here! I'm not convinced it's about foot fetishism. But I could be wrong.

The chugging guitars and marimba married to a slower rhythm slowly fade away. The whole piece is strangely melodic and catchy, and the Captain's voice, rather smooth.

'Petrified Forest' (Van Vliet)
We're pitched straight into the Captain's vision of the hellish future we're busy creating – a future where 'The carpet's wearing thin' and we'll soon be joining the dinosaurs in a petrified layer of rock. He's talking about the greedy who take but do not give back: 'Breathe in 'n' out hungry today 'n' eat hearty tomorrow/Or eat away 'n' be eaten some day'. He's saying that we must live in harmony in order to have any future.

Don was an environmentalist: an ecologist who clearly saw the dangers of our profit-driven polluting ways. Respect for nature and living in harmony are major themes running through his work – 'No flowers shall grow where oil shall flow', 'If the dinosaur cries with blood in his eyes/'N' eats our babies for our lies/Belch fire into our skies'. They're powerful words. If we continue to belch fire into the skies, we'll be part of the petrified forest. 'There'd be no game, brother, if no one would play'.

The music – just as harsh as the words – emphasises the sentiments. Chords are laden with doom, the sprinkling of marimba sounds desolate; bass and drum are ominous. The Captain's voice is tormented in a song that's stark and pitiless. For a moment, towards the end, his voice is mellow, but that soon relapses into grief. The bass-playing in the outro is extraordinary. What a song; a warning.

'One Red Rose That I Mean' (Instrumental) (Van Vliet)
Zoot Horn Rollo plays this amazing solo guitar number majestically. Don created it on piano, and Zoot carefully transcribed it for guitar. The complex and difficult composition is just under two minutes of exquisite music that bedazzles the ears and was written as a love offering to Don's wife Jan. Zoot's performance captures the melody and amorous emotion perfectly.

'The Buggy Boogie Woogie' (Van Vliet)
Another environmental gem, this time focussing on overpopulation, with an analogy of a spider and her thousands of offspring: 'I gotta keep sweepin' 'n' sweepin' 'fore they fill the room'. This turns from spiders to people: 'What this world needs now is a good two-dollar room 'n' a good two-dollar broom'/'N' there's still too many feet'.

The band sets up a funky blues groove, with Zoot's guitar creating a smooth bluesy refrain that's mellow and sweet. Drumbo displays his versatility with sensitive brushwork: delicate and soft, unlike his usual power. Rockette's bass is complex and sensual, adding a fluid jazz feel. Interestingly, the sweeping sound is Drumbo and Ed Marimba actually sweeping brooms over guitar cases. There is nothing atonal to be heard, no intricate polyrhythms, discordant sax or dissonance: just fabulous integrated blues. The vocal is perfection itself, starting with a gloriously deep baritone narration, and rising to a powerful blast that Howlin' Wolf would've been proud of: the occasional whoop and rise displaying the Captain's range.

It's an accessible stand-out track, reinforced with a clear message.

'The Smithsonian Institute Blues (Or The Big Dig)' (Van Vliet)

The environmental message is rammed home again with a poetic gem. The La Brea tar pits are a place in Los Angeles – an expanse of viscous liquid tar from which many well-preserved dinosaur skeletons have been recovered. The creatures became ensnared in the cloying tar. Many of these skeletons are displayed in the Smithsonian Institute. The analogy is made between dinosaurs and ourselves. We have inherited the world from them. They are now only a layer in rock. Is that our fate? Don thinks it is and has a bad dose of the Smithsonian Institute blues.

The bass and marimba intro is interesting. The band comes in with more wallop – guitars playing longer refrains than on *Trout Mask Replica*: less spiky but just as intricate. The bass and drums have a full sound. The marimba and lead guitar middle section is highly imaginative, with an entirely different feel to a standard rock song. Don is in fine voice – his initial deep growl interspersed with high inflections, rises as he puts his foot down and applies the power, ending with ominous bass tones.

'Space-Age Couple' (Van Vliet)

Yet another environmental warning from the Captain. It's becoming the album's major theme. The space-age couple are enslaved in modern-day life, working all hours in order to purchase trivia instead of really living. The Captain is exhorting them to wake up to the pollution in the world. He tells them there's a better way – to notice the wonders surrounding them, appreciate life, and live in harmony with the planet.

The track gallops along, riding on a cool repeating riff coupled with Drumbo's amazingly complicated drum rhythms, augmented by Ed Marinba's sparse percussion. The Captain's voice is full of urgency, urging and goading. The tempo changes and a different riff, meld with the hard-hitting lyrics. The music halts for a burst of marimba before Don proceeds into more forceful pleading.

I love this song but do find the backing muddy. More separation of the instruments would provide greater clarity. Much good music lies hidden in the mix.

'The Clouds Are Full Of Wine (Not Whiskey Or Rye)' (Van Vliet)

This has the same melody later used on 'Golden Birdies' from *Clear Spot*. The Captain's voice is mellow, smooth, crooning in a style I've never heard before. He sings rhymes dredged from the subliminal association that sound nonsensical yet capture elusive meaning. Verses are sung in a torrent: a never-broken stream. He barely pauses for breath, his voice rising and falling like rolling hills. The lyric intimates that you can get drunk on the sky's blueness, the rhinestone stars, the world teeming with life and mystery, and the sky with its infinite melodies that 'go on and on and on'.

The tempo is 4/4, but the first guitar is in 3/4. The duelling guitar and marimba have replaced the two guitars of previous albums, enabling a different intricate interplay, the bass between them acting as a foil, creating a three-way interweave. Fabulous. The drums come in adding power, supporting the vocal, a driving force to power the words through their sweeping verses.

The track's second half is instrumental – an amazing four-way interaction between Rockette, Zoot, Ed and Drumbo – melodic, changing, evolving, feeding off each other and ending with a burst of marimba to create a jazzy feast.

'Flash Gordon's Ape' (Van Vliet)

Don obviously wanted the album to finish with a splash, and that's what it does. What with Don's raucous atonal qualities, this is probably the track that persuaded Jan Van Vliet to hide his saxophones! It begins with a wall of tenor sax, so that when the band come in, they're almost completely buried under a hail of unruly squawks. I quite like the effect, but it is indeed highly discordant and hard on the ear. Hearing the track as it was later released without the sax, is a different experience altogether and less avant-garde. I think I prefer the chaos of the horns! They give it more bite. Without them the track is quite melodic but less extraordinary.

Juxtaposing the evolving guitar riff against marimba, bass and drums, provides a very different dynamic to any on *Trout Mask Replica*. The sophisticated marimba break is reminiscent of the first album's 'Dropout Boogie': a contrast that appeals to Don's creative invention.

As for the content, I think we're all Flash Gordon's apes, tearing around in outer space, pretending we're civilised, smart and knowledgeable. But we're just apes throwing bananas at the sun. 'The leaves are gettin' faker every day'. We think we're clever but, 'Your too day' (sic) – there might not be tomorrow.

The Spotlight Kid (1972)

Personnel:
Don Van Vliet 'Captain Beefheart': vocals, harmonica, jingle bells
John French 'Drumbo': drums, percussion
Bill Harkleroad 'Zoot Horn Rollo': guitar, slide guitar
Mark Boston 'Rockette Morton': bass
Art Tripp 'Ed Marimba/Ted Cactus': drums, percussion, marimba, piano, harpsichord
Elliot Ingber 'Winged Eel Fingerling': guitar on 'I'm gonna Booglarize You, Baby' and 'Alice In Blunderland'.
Rhys Clark: drums on 'Glider'
Producers: Don Van Vliet, Phil Schier
Recorded at the Record Plant, Los Angeles
Ed Thrasher: photography and cover artwork
Label: Reprise

After two brilliant albums of inventive avant-garde rock music, but without tasting success, the Captain was experiencing a change of heart. He'd woken up to the fact that innovative experimental music might satisfy the creative soul but wasn't putting bread on the table. No money was coming in. He reassessed.

The band had gone back to communal living – first near Ben Lomond in California, then further north in Trinidad, North California. Soon, the bad old ways returned, as Don started to impose himself on the younger members. There was a return to tyrannical control, victimisation, bullying and psychological warfare, sometimes even escalating into levels of previously unseen physical violence. For some reason, the worst was directed at Zoot Horn Rollo. On one occasion, he was actually thrown into a dumpster. Money was scarce; the band was dependent on welfare checks and contributions from relatives. They were really suffering for their art.

Don's answer to the financial predicament was to consciously simplify the music. He slowed it down, removing the avant-garde elements to make it more mainstream and accessible. To an extent, they went back to being a blues band: but with something extra. Don craved success and was now prepared to compromise. The band hated it. After experiencing the heights of artistic creativity, they found this new style simple, undemanding and too damn slow. This simplified playing proved to be boring. They craved the complexities and demands of the previous style.

Strangely, I loved it. While it doesn't hit the wonders of invention and experimentation that were *Trout Mask Replica* and Lick My Decals Off, Baby, it is heavy, and redolent with great performances, brilliant lyrics and themes that I could identify with. They were all there: the sexuality, environmentalism, pacifism. While this might've been simpler, it was still most definitely Beefheart of the highest calibre. The fundamental elements were there in the poetry, the incredible voice and brilliant musicianship. What wasn't to like?

Though Jeff 'Antennae Jimmy Semens' Cotton had – sadly – not returned to resume his incredible guitar attack with Zoot, there were still two duelling guitars. The Captain brought in Elliot 'Winged Eel Fingerling' Ingber on three of the ten tracks to reinstate that much-loved element. A good sign. Rather bemusingly, the album was credited to Captain Beefheart with no mention of the Magic Band at all. That seemed like ego gone mad to me. It was tantamount to The Rolling Stones calling themselves Mick Jagger.

For the live touring, Alex St. Clair was brought back into the fold. In my opinion, this was probably the Magic Band's best lineup, and I was fortunate to catch them at The Rainbow in London in 1973. Rockette Morton came out with what looked like a space helmet on his head. He said 'Hi, I'm Rockette Morton. I'm just here to do a toast', and laughed. He then threw the helmet off and proceeded to perform this amazing solo while pogoing all over the stage. Many years later, I was in conversation with Mark (Rockette) and asked him about the helmet. He laughed and told me it was a big old American toaster. His intro suddenly made sense. He told me the band had come through the airport in their stage gear and he was wearing the toaster – the British customs officer never blinked or said a word.

At The Rainbow, towards the end of his solo, the band came out and plugged in. They then performed the brilliant instrumental 'Suction Prints' ('Pompadour Swamp' as it was then called). It was searing. The two guitars burned white hot. The drums and bass, with their crazy rhythm, powered the band into a different dimension. With his long hair flailing, Zoot was majestic as he scattered bursts of molten slide guitar. Alex 'St. Clair' Snouffer duelled exquisitely with Zoot on guitar and slide. They blew my socks off. As if that wasn't enough (By now, we were all on our feet and down at the front, bopping ecstatically), this incredible voice boomed out from the wings. I remembered it as 'Electricity', but the bootlegs of the gig show it was really *Mirror Man*'. The power of the voice was frightening. The Captain walked on stage to a massive roar. What followed was one of the best gigs ofn my life: up there with Jimi Hendrix, Cream, Roy Harper and Pink Floyd.

'I'm Gonna Booglarize You Baby' (Van Vliet)

The album starts with a slice of rich voodoo swamp music: a gumbo of soupy blues laced with raunch. The bass throbs through your gut with amazing seminal force. The guitars assault your ears with slashing riffs. It's a visceral slab of basic gut-wrenching blues that harks back to *Mirror Man*. It's great to hear those guitars gelling so well, with Winged Eel Fingerling slotting right in, playing that E7 riff. Zoot and Fingerling may be playing slower, simpler riffs, but they're still as effective as on the *Trout Mask Replica* duelling.

Don's voice is a deep sexy growl. There's no doubt he's intending to booglarize you, baby, like nobody's been booglarized before. With his menacing, dark, brooding sexuality, this is primeval sex. You can taste it. This ain't no love song.

In the lyric, a couple are driving around with a Cajun moon reflecting off the hood of their car. They're hot for sex, but there's nowhere to stop. She invites him back to her place and promises to slow his motor down. She's gonna booglarize him real good. Woah. This is right up there with the best!

'White Jam' (Van Vliet)

Here there is a change to a light and sweet mood, with delicate keyboards from Ed Marimba. Even the Captain's voice is gentle and laid-back. The tone may be different to the first track, but the subject matter is the same. We're still talking sex here, with what is surely a subtle ode to oral sex. Making love in the fields under the sunshine; making love at night with her scent and those yams driving him crazy.

The second half undergoes a change with the blues harp panting, Don is high on pleasure, his voice rising in ecstasy. He doesn't know where he is, but I think we're getting close to white jam time.

'Blabber 'N Smoke' (Van Vliet, Jan Van Vliet)

The world's in a mess and 'All you ever do is blabber and smoke'. Jan wrote this in frustration with Don. According to Jan, all Don ever did was sit around moaning and smoking without doing anything.

There are some great lines interspersed with simple, effective allusions: 'There's a pain in your window'. 'Clean up the air/Treat the animals fair'. The pain is the damage we're doing. The remedy is simple: start looking after nature.

We're back to the guitar/marimba sound of Decals here. The music is not standard Beefheart: this is a slow, languid piece. Steady drums, bass and lazy guitar create a sleepy feeling. The track sits well with me. It's music to get stoned to.

'When It Blows Its Stacks' (Van Vliet)

If anyone was in danger of nodding off during the last track, this one would wake them up. We're back to that sleazy swamp, with enough menace to send your spine-tingling, heart racing and to chill your blood. This is like a lysergic version of Howlin' Wolf's 'Backdoor Man', played with a heavy E chord.

He's a ladies man. He's cold and calculated like a snake. He takes what he wants and doesn't hang around. I bet this guy 'eats more chicken than any man ever seen', but when there's trouble, he's nowhere to be found.

The heavy bass line sets the momentum. We're ploughing through the murk on a juggernaut. The Captain is groaning, growling, moaning and howlin' like the Wolf on a trip. The guitar oozes a slow sleazy riff, interspersed with searing bursts of lead. The marimba does a tango with the bass until the guitar butts in and blows them away. Ominous chords rumble real slow as the Captain wails. Watch out, you girls; there's an old man-eater around.

'Alice In Blunderland' (Van Vliet)

Side one ends with a four-minute instrumental that feels a tad short. Marimba, hefty bass lines, exquisite drum patterns and heavy chords meld to create a unique base. The band keep up their heavy lurching rhythm while Winged Eel Fingerling takes centre stage. The rhythm is a solid platform for him to let fly. He soars off into an inspired lead solo that melts the strings: not so much technique as sheer passion and creativity.

'The Spotlight Kid' (Van Vliet)

This is an opaque, fun poem packed with elusive meaning and all manner of metaphor. Is Spotlight Kid a female Jesus on the mountain with her fishes and loaves, never showing for her second coming, dispensing alibis in the latest fashion? Or is she a metaphor for mankind, trying to be trendy and important while eating everything in sight? Perhaps Mother Nature? Or perhaps this is just Don playing with words, his rockin' chair groaning like a grizzly bear.

The first stanza has him singing solo. When the band plays, they compliment him in perfect harmony. The guitar, bass and marimba meld together, perfectly synchronised. Slow and languid drums create a unique sound that evolves into a melodic swing, with the marimba giving a Latin feel. There's a short bass solo before Don's voice – rising and falling – delivers the poem in deep expressive tones.

The guitar becomes gutsier, the drum roll aggressive, threatening to motor forward but then faltering, slipping back into that gentle sound. Towards the end, Don sings some high notes before the song comes to its conclusion. Fun and intriguing.

'Click Clack' (Van Vliet)

This has all the makings of a classic blues track but with a Beefheart twist. It starts in 3/4 time and goes into 4/4 with brain-frizzling syncopation. The slide, harmonica, guitar and bass slip into a mind-boggling groove that supremely captures the swaying of a train on the tracks.

The Captain is doing his own 'Smokestack Lightning' – it's a tale of his girl leaving him on a train to New Orleans in search of excitement. For two years, she's been leaving and returning on the two railway tracks. This time it looks like she's going for good, and he's down on the ground, praying for the train to stop as she waves her handkerchief out the window.

Piano sets up a rhythm for the bass, which drives it along. Visceral slide guitar wails like a train whistle. The Captain is laden with desperation as he watches the train disappearing into the distance. The bass pounds as the band apply more power, driving you crazy as the train speeds away. In muffled tones, the Captain asks whether we've 'ever had a girl like that', as he treats us to great harmonica-playing. The slide guitar sounds like it's waving goodbye as the train disappears.

'Grow Fins' (Van Vliet)

Another great accessible blues track with a railroad rhythm. Don's blues voice would put Chester Burnett to shame. Once again, you're never quite sure how to take the lyric. Should it be taken literally? Does it describe Don and Jan arguing, throwing food around on the walls, draining board and floor? Or was it more general – a relationship going wrong, no hugs or love; the house in a mess? 'You know how to act, but you're giving me the blues'. Or is this a metaphor for mankind and the mess we're making of the planet? Maybe it's all three. Don's voice is majestic, and in the middle section, his harmonica plays a solo against the guitar and marimba. In the louder parts, there's a lot going on, but often the instruments are indistinct, the music hidden in the mix. Mostly the track is pared back with harp and bass dominant, drums steady and a repetitive groove that sucks you in.

'There Ain't No Santa Claus On The Evenin' Stage' (Van Vliet)

I always picture the Biafra famine when I hear this track. This slow blues shows Don at his compassionate best. He growls, wails and moans his way through this classic, his voice grief-stricken and desolate. The slow, plodding bass sets the tone with dashes of ironic sleigh bells creating a mesmeric dirge. A mournful slide guitar plays a repeating refrain, snarly and stark, facing off against a second guitar that's quieter in and playing a different coda. Is that slide screeching 'No Santa Claus', or is that just me?

There's a metallic earthy grit to the backing. Don growls in his lowest register. There's no help coming. Despair rises as his voice takes on an agonised tone. The wail of a doleful harmonica, signals hopelessness. The 'Ho ho ho' mantra is full of satirical pathos. The guitar in the background sounds out a death knell with chilling virtuosity.

'Glider' (Van Vliet)

You couldn't end the album on such a bleak tone as 'There Ain't No Santa Claus On The Evenin' Stage', brilliant though it was, could you? 'Glider' may be a slow blues, but at least it's in an upward direction. The song shows how the *Trout Mask Replica*-era band had moved away from using psychedelics, and into meditation. The blues are the sweeping skies reflecting a state of peace and a quiet retreat from the noise and chaos of the world. Don and Jan are in a world of their own. Better knock on wood, there's thunder and lightnin'; getting pretty frightening down here, but up in the clouds it's peaceful and serene.

'Glider' starts with a slow wailing harmonica. It's another brooding slow blues. It sounds much like Drumbo playing those complex rhythms, but in actual fact, it's Rhys Clark.

To me, the vocal has a desolate feel. The harmonica plays throughout. The slide guitar slices its way into a biting solo, then duelling with a fainter second slide, returning to synch up with the drums, bass and harmonica before hitting an abrupt end.

Clear Spot (1972)

Personnel:
Don Van Vliet 'Captain Beefheart': vocals, harmonica
Bill Harkleroad 'Zoot Horn Rollo': guitar, slide guitar, mandolin
Roy Estrada 'Orejon' 'Big Ears': bass
Mark Boston 'Rockette Morton': rhythm guitar and bass on 'Golden Birdies'
Art Tripp 'Ed Marimba/Ted Cactus': drums, percussion, marimba, piano, harpsichord
Milt Holland: percussion
Russ Titelman: guitar on 'Too Much Time'
Jerry Jumonville: horn arrangement on 'Too Much Time'
Don Van Vliet and Ted Templeton: horn arrangement on 'Long Neck Bottles' & 'Woman's Got To Hit A Man'
The Blackberries: backing vocals
Producer: Ted Templeton
Engineer: Donn Landee
Recorded at Amigo Studios, Los Angeles
Ed Thrasher: art direction
Jim McCrary: photography
John and Barbara Casado: design
Label: Reprise

After the experimental/avant-garde music of *Trout Mask Replica* and Lick My Decals Off, Baby, Don had produced the more accessible *The Spotlight Kid*, which was a return to his blues roots. It was not by chance that *Clear Spot* was later released on CD along with *The Spotlight Kid*. *Clear Spot* is a continuation of that style, and much of the material was written at the same time. The two albums were created while the Magic Band was together in Felton and Trinidad, California. Once again, the personnel had changed. John French had bitten the dust: Artie Tripp taking over on drums, and even Mark Boston was largely eclipsed by Roy Estrada from The Mothers Of Invention.

Don was hungry for success. He'd seen that the far-out avant-garde style was never going to break through into the mainstream. Recognising this, he'd reverted to a simpler, blues-based style on *The Spotlight Kid*, but that hadn't brought success either. Swallowing his pride, he stepped down from production and brought in the seasoned team of Templeton and Landee. They'd proved themselves by creating successful records for Van Morrison and The Doobie Brothers. Don hoped the team might work their magic for him. In an attempt to achieve commercial success, they continued the accessible style already established on *The Spotlight Kid*, augmented with a horn section. Unfortunately, it was a complete failure. The album failed to chart in the UK and only reached 191 on *Billboard*. Though the album received favourable reviews, sales were poor – the reason being that the band didn't tour to promote the album. They only played a few local gigs.

Left: The cover of the *A&M Sessions*, the 1965 release of the entire five-track session of the two singles with an unreleased track. *(A&M)*

Right: *Safe As Milk* – the 1967 classic debut which mixed blues with psychedelia. *(Buddah)*

Left: *Mirror Man* – the four brilliant and elongated blues jams that showed just what the Magic Band of 1965 and 1966 sounded like. *(Buddah)*

Right: *Strictly Personal* – the controversial 1968 album with psychedelic phasing. (*Blue Thumb*)

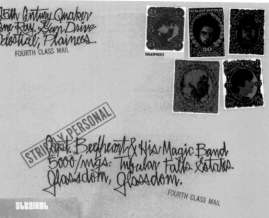

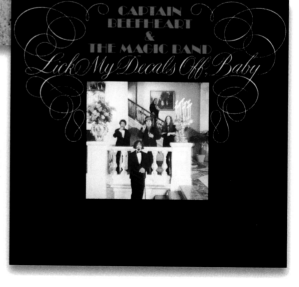

Left: *Trout Mask Replica* – the 1969 experimental masterpiece that was way ahead of its time. (*Straight*)

Right: *Lick My Decals Off, Baby* – the 1970 album that consolidated the *Trout Mask* experiment. (*Straight*)

Left: Captain Beefheart at the Town Hall in 1975. (*Vinnie Vincent*)

Right: At the Bottom Line in New York in 1974. (*Vinnie Vincent*)

Right: Another shot from the Bottom Line in 1974. (*Vinnie Vincent*)

Below: Captain Beefheart with Artie Tripp. (*Stanley Prover*)

Left: *Spotlight Kid* – the 1972 move to a bluesy, simpler style. (*Reprise*)

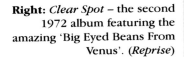

Right: *Clear Spot* – the second 1972 album featuring the amazing 'Big Eyed Beans From Venus'. (*Reprise*)

Left: *Unconditionally Guaranteed* – the 1974 attempt at a commercial direction that caused the band to leave Don. (*Virgin*)

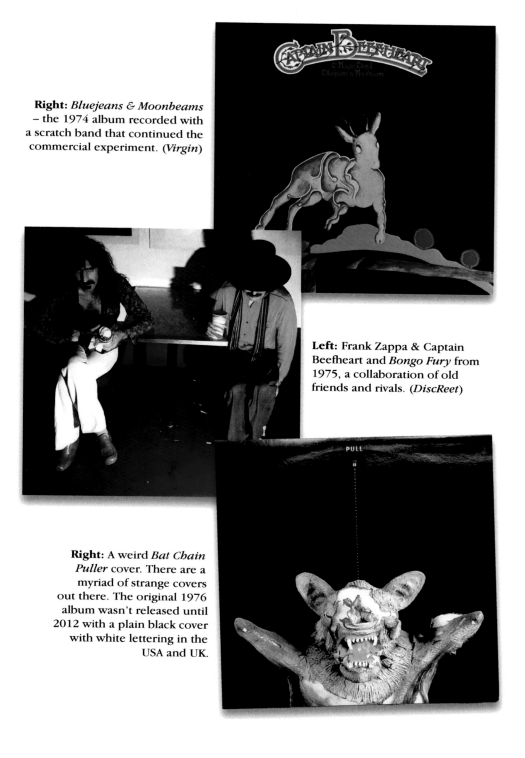

Right: *Bluejeans & Moonbeams* – the 1974 album recorded with a scratch band that continued the commercial experiment. (*Virgin*)

Left: Frank Zappa & Captain Beefheart and *Bongo Fury* from 1975, a collaboration of old friends and rivals. (*DiscReet*)

Right: A weird *Bat Chain Puller* cover. There are a myriad of strange covers out there. The original 1976 album wasn't released until 2012 with a plain black cover with white lettering in the USA and UK.

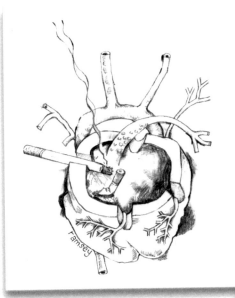

Left: 'Ashtray Heart' drawing; an illustration for the 1980 *Doc At The Radar* album track 'Ashtray Heart' – 'You used me like an ashtray heart. Case of the punks. Right from the start'. (*Ramsay Williamson*)

Right: 'Fast And Bulbous' drawing; an illustration of the famous quote from *Trout Mask Replica* album – 'A squid eating dough in a polyethene bag is fast 'n' bulbous, got me?' (*Ramsay Williamson*)

Left: 'Black Ants' drawing – Ramsay's illustration of Don's quote about music notation 'Music is just black ants crawling across white paper'. (*Ramsay Williamson*)

Above: Captain Beefheart with Gary Lucas in 1980. *(Courtesy of Gary Lucas)*

Left: Captain Beefheart in 1975. *(Neil Sharrow)*

Right: Captain Beefheart in 1975 once again. *(Neil Sharrow)*

© 1975 Neil Sharrow
lastsafari@fuse.net

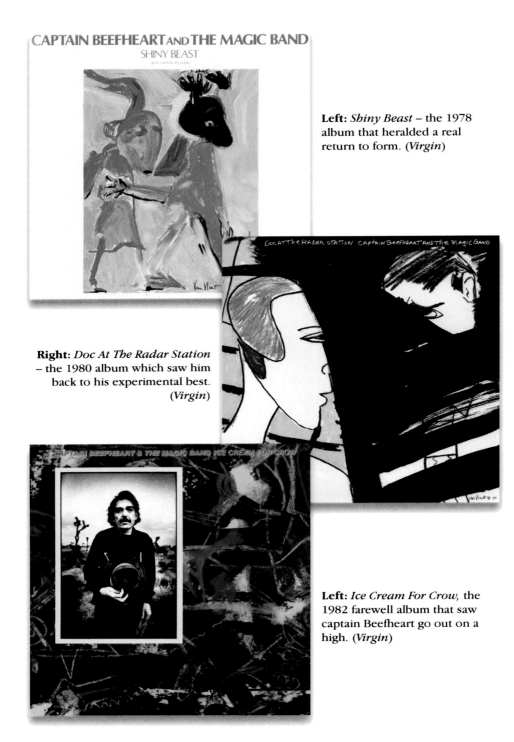

Left: *Shiny Beast* – the 1978 album that heralded a real return to form. (*Virgin*)

Right: *Doc At The Radar Station* – the 1980 album which saw him back to his experimental best. (*Virgin*)

Left: *Ice Cream For Crow,* the 1982 farewell album that saw captain Beefheart go out on a high. (*Virgin*)

The Magic Band in 2005 – Gary 'Mantis' Lucas, John 'Drumbo' French, Mark 'Rockette Morton' Boston and Denny 'Feelers Rebo' Walley. (*Opher Goodwin*)

Left: The author with Rockette Morton in 2005. (*Liz Goodwin*)

The Magic Band 2005 – John 'Drumbo' French, Rockette Morton and Denny Walley. (*Opher Goodwin*)

Left: *Mirror Man* – The German cover from 1971. Not as good a concept as the smashed mirror idea. (*Buddah*)

Right: 'Plastic Factory' – the cover for the 7" single from 2012 with the B-side 'Where There's Woman'. (*Buddah*)

Left: 'Upon The My-O-My' – the 1974 single taken from the *Unconditionally Guaranteed* album. The B-side is 'I Got Love On My Mind'. (*Sundazed/Mercury*)

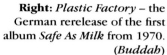

Right: *Plastic Factory* – the German rerelease of the first album *Safe As Milk* from 1970. (*Buddah*)

Left: *Don's Birthday Party* – An unofficial European release of a double live album. The concert was recorded live on January 15, 1981, at the Showboat Theatre in Seattle – a celebration of Don's 40th birthday.

Right: *Another Chapter From The Life And Times Of Captain Beefheart*. A 1989 unofficial German double album. It features the 1966 Avalon ballroom gig plus an assortment of sessions and outtakes. (*Archive Productions*)

Above: The Magic Band in Leeds in 2017 – Eric Klerks gets into it! (*Opher Goodwin*)

Left: The Magic Band in Leeds in 2017 again – Eric Klerks and John 'Drumbo' French feeding off each other musically. (*Opher Goodwin*)

The Magic Band in Leeds, four years earlier in 2013 – John 'Drumbo' French blows some Beefheartian sax while Rockette looks on and Craig Bunch is on the drums. (*Opher Goodwin*)

Above: The Magic Band in Lincoln in 2014. Eric Klerks on slide guitar and Rockette Morton is on bass while John 'Drumbo' French gives it his all. (*Opher Goodwin*)

Right: The Magic Band at Leeds Irish Centre in 2017 – John 'Drumbo' French enjoys himself with Henry Kuttner in the background. (*Opher Goodwin*)

The Magic Band in Lincoln in 2014 – Denny 'Feelers Rebo' Walley hits the high notes. (*Opher Goodwin*)

Left: A rare poster for *Safe As Milk*.

Right: A signed Magic Band Farewell Tour poster from the Irish Centre in Leeds in 2017. (*The Opher Goodwin collection*)

As far as die-hard Beefheart fans were concerned, the album was yet another triumph. I remember rushing home to play it, and again being completely blown away: vintage Beef. Little did I know of the mind games, victimisation and bullying that had returned to plague the band as Don continued his tricks to mould them. He had a vision, and musicians were merely the tools he deployed. Because of his age, ability, reputation, persona and contacts, they held him in awe and tolerated the domineering.

Don often referred to the Earth as God's golfball and set up a company by that name with his manager Grant Gibbs and their accountant. The band were signed as employees, ostensibly to receive royalties via the company. However, they received tax bills but no money and that contract later became a noose around their necks.

The album title was originally Brown Star before they settled on *Clear Spot*. The cover is a story in itself. Don started with grandiose plans. He managed to convince Reprise Records that he was a viable commercial prospect worth investing in. The cover needed to be something different and eye-catching. His original concept was to produce a clear plastic sleeve with the title *Clear Spot* embossed on the front. The album was to be made of transparent vinyl with no inner sleeve. There was going to be an insert with a black-and-white band photo in what looked like a space-age studio control panel, but what, in reality, was the band playing with the controls at the Griffin Park Observatory. The photo had calibrations along two sides to enhance the weird science effect, with Beefheart peering out in a Chinese coolie hat. The insert would display the name Captain Beefheart and The Magic Band, track details and credits. But for financial reasons, the transparent vinyl never happened, and subsequent reissues reverted to conventional sleeves.

The title, *Clear Spot,* could be a description of Don's wish to find a comfortable place away from people and society. But at the time, there was a type of LSD making the rounds; a microdot going by the name of *Clear Spot*: which does beg the question. In the media, Don was trying to distance himself from drugs, claiming that he and the band never took them and that you could get high and reach a spiritual state through natural means. Zoot claims that when he joined the band, they were into meditation, so there could be some truth to this.

The recording of the album went well, but Zoot and others have commented that this new formula of slower, blues-based songs was too simple and boring. After the complexity of Trout and Decals, there was no challenge.

In addition to *Clear Spot*'s double-CD release with *The Spotlight Kid*, and various vinyl reissues, it was included with Decals and Spotlight – along with an album of outtakes – in Rhino Records' Sun Zoom Spark box set in 2015.

'Low Yo Yo Stuff' (Van Vliet)

Straight into the raw sex of a raunchy blues number that sounds as if it comes churning out of the Mississippi swamp. Starting with a low dirty guitar riff, syncopated drums and fluid bass, it creates a heavy grinding sound reminiscent of the blues sound of Jay Miller's production for Ernie Young's Louisiana label Excello. It's more accessible than the avant-garde of Trout and Decals, but every bit as powerful and moving.

I would like to hear a clearer, crisper production with more separation. There is a lot going on in the background, but, sadly, fabulous slide guitar, marimba and other instruments are partially lost in the muddy sound created the arrangement. Despite this gripe, the music projects a really dirty blues effect with real energy. Zoot's guitar solo is slow and restrained with clear chiming notes. Now that he's not blasting out notes in crazy patterns and rhythms, he's more focused on each note's sound.

Sex is a major theme of Don's poems, and this is one of his best. He uses 'yo yo' in various ways: from a girl's use of her sexuality, to a guy's masturbation. 'Whether you're old, young, rich, poor, tall or skinny/Everybody's doing it'.

'Nowadays A Woman's Gotta Hit A Man' (Van Vliet)
This song is unadulterated feminism seen from the male point of view. Don Van Vliet:

> There's been a big ecological imbalance for years, what with women taking a back seat to men for so long. Their influence on life has been mutated, and because of it, the men have been getting into wars and screwing things up. My inspiration comes from appreciating women for what they are.

For once, the lyrics are clear without ambiguity.

There's a drum's pounding rhythm as Ed Marimba of the green moustache lays down a heavy base for the others to latch on to. The bass, guitars and a wailing blues harp come in and we're straight into an electric blues. The song evolves with great complexity. Brass overshadows but adds an interesting dimension. You win something, you lose something. The slide guitar solo at 2:05 is searing and majestic: Elmore James never attempted anything quite like this. At times, notes splatter in quick-time volleys. Fabulous.

This is a contrast to the complex polyrhythms and varying time signatures of other albums, and yet it's sublime. I was unsure which I preferred and finally decided they are equally brilliant. At times, the production creates a wall of noise that ebbs and flows. As much as I like the overall sound, I would still like to hear the individual contributions more clearly.

It's a rollicking track with an important message that continues the album's social thrust.

'Too Much Time' (Van Vliet)
This complete change of style doesn't sound like the Magic Band. It's a soulful rendition. Don is doing his best Otis Redding and could be straight out of Stax or Motown. This is mainstream soul – so radio-friendly it could've easily been

a major hit. Don is sitting (on the dock of the bay?), whimsically pondering the beauties of nature and the follies of man. He's eating crackers and sardines, pining for a woman to love, someone to share his reverie and cook for him. He's got so much love to share.

The guitar/bongos intro leads into a full band complete with horns – that could've come straight out of McLemore Ave in Memphis. There's a smooth-talking section and even a girl chorus!

It's beautifully done, but I wasn't sure I liked it at first – it's so un-Beefheart – but I came around. It reminds me of 'I'm Glad' from *Safe As Milk*, but it's more polished.

'Circumstances' (Van Vliet)
Now we're straight back into vintage Beefheart with the full force unleashed. The vocal is dynamic, blasting the speakers like on 'Electricity'. It packs a hefty wallop. Don forcefully preaches that only once you've realised the circumstances (the way this world is run by a bunch of old greedy warmongers), are you fit to go out into it. He exhorts us to remember, that the sun can burn you, but not as bad as those old folk. If you have the understanding that the universe is wonderful and love is the most important goal, then you are equipped. Take care.

Starting with a slow guitar, the song proceeds with a wailing harmonica before the band kicks in with punchy drums and slide guitar in a driving rhythm. This is not quite blues and not quite the music of Decals, but it's getting there. There is incredible variation and dynamics here, adding to the song's strength. Towards the end, every molecule of air from Don's lungs streams through those hoary vocal cords. The band plays a compelling slow harmonica-driven riff before shuddering to an abrupt halt. That sure blows away any cobwebs.

'My Head Is My Only House Unless It Rains' (Van Vliet)
I never thought I'd ever be describing any Beefheart track as tender and beautiful, but this song is as poignant a ballad as you'll ever get. Look out, girl; the Captain's on the prowl looking for a soulmate. He's not going to rest until he's hunted her down and beguiled her with the sweetness of his song. He may have to take a train or even a plane if she's too far away, but he's not going to eat, sleep or take shelter (unless it rains!) until he can wrap his arms around her. I've never heard Don sing so beautifully. It's a slow ballad with conventional backing. He's crooning. The guitar purrs. It's just a sweetly sung poem in an orthodox format that would not be out of place on late-night radio.

'Sun Zoom Spark' (Van Vliet)
Now Don smashes us with all the aggression and fury of a tornado, and we're caught up in a burst of light, zoom and spark. This sound is straight back to Don's trademark psychedelic blues with dirty riffs, duelling guitars and shrill

slide guitar. There's even an evil dose of harmonica. He pumps everything into his vocal, spitting out words in a gushing stream, using his full, mighty range.

Right from the opening guitar chords, you know you're in for a treat. Zoot provides blistering slide, up and down the frets. The bass line is exquisite. The music's got everything.

This is one of Don's ambiguous poems that allow your imagination to run riot. It gives you a glimmer of understanding, but the meaning remains just out of reach. The music is magic, and the lyrics connect sunrise to guitars – describing infinity's universal magnet drawing light from the dark and music from the guitar. Everything is endless. 'Does it start at the bottom? Or does it start at the top? Hope it don't stop'. Stop it does. We're at the end of side one.

'Clear Spot' (Van Vliet)
Wrrrrrrr!!! Back to the dirtiest nitty-gritty of swampy blues, in a straightforward 4/4 time, churning the muddy waters into a rich aural soup. The band is caught in a cement mixer, slowly swirling through a riff-driven, meaty, savoury sound that throbs through your guts to the very essence of primordial being; so primitive you can sense the caveman stir. The Captain was sick of the mess being made in a world vastly overpopulated, but not with people he could relate to. He wanted somewhere to live away from humanity's foolishness: a *Clear Spot*.

That evil guitar riff begins the piece. The bass sets up a repeating refrain. The voice is clear and dramatic as the tension builds. There's some underpinning slide guitar. The first section ends with a long-extended note before the band crashes back in with a gut-wrenching rhythm. The drums thud in the chorus, and the harp wails in misery. A well-annunciated Don exhorts us to feel his torment as he searches for the way out. With a last fantastic elongated descending slide guitar note, we are out of there.

'Crazy Little Thing' (Van Vliet)
The pace doesn't let up with 'Crazy Little Thing', as the song lives up to its name. Right from the first guitar, there's a feeling of expectation: perhaps it's that E-major with plenty of right-hand power. The Captain and band jump in with the force of a tornado, propelling us into the stratosphere. The sound jumps right out at us. The forceful voice is incredibly powerful, fusing with the percussion and riffing guitars. The bass line is the engine room. The snatch of girl chorus and the call-and-response technique work beautifully.

Right from the start, this song motors on maximum impact. It has all the guitar hallmarks of a top-notch Beefheart track. I love the way those two nasty-sounding guitars work off each other, exchanging riffs and licks; one sliding up and one down.

This should've been a hit because it's classic hard rock, but perhaps a song about jailbait might've been a tad too much for popular consumption. When Bowie sang about those pretty things driving their mothers and fathers insane, he was describing how some young girls can flaunt their burgeoning sexuality. Beefheart describes a particular coquettish girl in a far more raunchy way.

'Long Neck Bottles' (Van Vliet)

Side two is relentless, with a more-bluesy feel, some great harmonica-playing and sharp power chords. In his best narrating mode, Don tells the story of a hard-living woman. He doesn't normally talk about his women, but in this case, he made an exception. She was a hard case who could hold her own with any man and drink them under the table. She's sure tough. She's wild. She once got high and shot up the town: 'I'll be damned if she didn't bring an airplane down'. Now he's sung about her, he's gonna have to get out of town.

There's a relentless funky rhythm. Guitars exchange raunchy chords while Don plays harmonica and brags about his woman's exploits. The band takes us into the seediest bar in town.

'Her Eyes Are a Blue Million Miles' (Van Vliet)

Finally, we get to cool it a little, with this beautiful love song. Although delicate and melodic, it somehow displays many Beefheart elements. The fabulous drum rhythm holds it all together. Guitars are riffing and interchanging, but this time with a gentle beauty. The bass line is a funky backbone for the instruments to hang from. The voice is achingly soft as the guitars repeat the flowing, dreamy riff. 'Her eyes are a blue million miles', and the band's wafting notes lead us on as we fall into a tender infinite whirlpool.

The Coen Brothers featured this track in their 1998 film *The Big Lebowski*.

'Big Eyed Beans from Venus' (Van Vliet)

Just when you've caught your breath, Don hits you with a surreal blaster. It's probably the greatest track the Magic Band ever recorded. It's a showstopper. I remember seeing them perform this in 1973 at the Rainbow in London, and it completely blew my mind. When Mr.Zoot Horn Rollo plays all 15 seconds of that long note, it still sends shivers through me. Does music get any better than this?

The Captain said, 'There are only 40 people in the world and five of them are hamburgers'. I guess he meant they were just meat walking around. He found it hard to find people he could relate to and engage with. As he says in the song: 'There's a limited supply'. To most people, he was some weird alien. Now he's suggesting that we aliens should unite: 'Beam in on me, baby and we'll beam together'. We're all related 'Distant cousins', and we sure can open our minds and purchase some of these magic beans from Venus. We can glow. We can 'get on the right track'. It's not confusion. Just open those big eyes to the universe. Acid or meditation, it matters little. This is about expanding minds so that the weird becomes normal. Get a load of those beans.

From the beginning, we're on a journey with those two guitars exchanging jagged chords. In the most expansive voice, the Captain talks as a brief drum pattern breaks in. Then the band introduces itself with supreme confidence. A minute in, there's a pause as Don exhorts Zoot to deliver that famous long spine-chilling lunar note – hanging and building as the track breaks into top gear, the band letting fly, drums flailing, bass booming, guitars raging. 'Ain't no SNAFU', the Captain tells us. The track takes off into orbit, returning to Earth, with an outro of slashing chords and another long note left hanging in the air.

This is Beefheart at his best; the best track of the album, if not of his whole career. How do you follow that?

'Golden Birdies' (Van Vliet)

This is very different and like a return to the experimentation of *Trout Mask Replica*, only slicker. It's a poem with minimal backing. Beginning with a single line and a brief burst of music, what follows is poetry interspersed with carefully synchronised marimba and guitar. Two full-blooded spurts of the full band jump in to emphasise important lines.

The poem is a bizarre creation, full of surreal mysticism and fabricated words that defy rational interpretation yet imply meaning just beyond the grasp of our comprehension. 'Shish sookie singabus'. With magical spiritual symbolism from the Obi-man shaman, the poem speaks of alternative layers of reality in which he releases 'golden birdies' as he snores.

Amazingly, it works perfectly, completes the album, and is the ideal adjunct to 'Big Eyed Beans From Venus'. Nothing else would work. 'Webcor Webcor'.

Unconditionally Guaranteed (1974)

Personnel:
Don Van Vliet 'Captain Beefheart': vocals, blues harp
Alex St. Clair Snouffer: guitar
Bill Harkleroad 'Zoot Horn Rollo': guitar, bottleneck guitar
Mark Boston 'Rockette Morton': bass
Artie Tripp 'Ed Marimba': drums, percussion
Mark Marcellino: keyboards
Andy DiMartino: acoustic guitar
Del Simmons: tenor saxophone, flute
Producer: Andy DiMartino
Engineers: John Guess, Jim Callon
Recorded at Hollywood Sound
Susanne Ayers: photography
Des Strobel: art direction
Terry Squire: design
Label: Virgin (UK), Mercury (USA)

The two previous albums had been simpler, less adventurous, and blues-based. Nevertheless, I rated them highly and was greatly looking forward to this one. The lineup of musicians was the same, but I could hear that the music had been smoothed over and the magic was missing. It sounded too mainstream and even lacked the blues edge of the last two. I guess nobody transcribed those edgy piano parts the way that John French and Bill Harkleroad did in the past. This was pop, and I found it very confusing. The band had an even more negative view of the album. They were appalled, considering it to be a sellout and an insult. For them, it was the last straw. They were sick of receiving no money and being bullied and abused. They walked out.

Don now found himself contracted for a tour, just weeks away, but he had no band. With the help of the DiMartinos, he hurriedly assembled a group of able musicians and put them through an intensive learning experience. Within a matter of days, they had to learn enough of the Magic Band repertoire to perform a concert.

Of course, I had no knowledge of all this and had been getting excited at the prospect of seeing the Magic Band again. In 1973, they'd delivered what was probably the best gig I'd ever been to. I now coerced many of my friends – even those who'd never heard of Beefheart – to buy tickets and come and see for themselves.

I had great memories of the show I'd seen and was really excited about seeing the Magic Band again. But when we arrived at the gig, I discovered that – except for Don of course – the band was made up of complete unknowns. I was initially crestfallen. Where I was expecting to see the fabulous Zoot, there was Fuzzy Fuscaldo on guitar; instead of Rockette, there was Paul Uhrig on bass, Ty Grimes on drums, Dean Smith on guitar and Del Simmons on

71

saxophone and flute. All unknown to me. However, the band had endured numerous personnel changes, and every previous incarnation had been excellent, so why not this one? I was ready to give them a shot. But sadly – as far as I was concerned – the gig was a travesty. Everything was so smoothed out that the songs sounded like standard rock numbers. They were no different from any other band. They lacked all the excitement, adventure and power of the Magic Band that I knew. There was no weaving-guitar magic, searing slide or fractious patterns. Even the best songs were bland. The Captain – who seemed to be trying everything possible – just couldn't pull it up out of the quagmire of ordinary. Rarely have I been more disappointed. Ironically, my friends all loved it.

Among Beefheart fans, the band rapidly became known as the Tragic Band. We were quick to spot a sellout when we saw one. Not that the Captain admitted as much. Throughout the tour, he'd been quick to defend both the band and the equally disappointing album, although he later disowned the album and told everyone to ask for their money back.

Meanwhile, the original disgruntled Magic Band members – unable for contractual reasons to use either the band name or their stage names – began gigging and putting some ideas together. Don was desperate and tried to coax both John French and Bill Harkleroad back by offering them producer roles on the next album. But they were having none of it.

These disaffected band members were trying out new songs and personnel. At first, John French returned to the fold as singer. That idea didn't work out. Eventually – with the help of Jethro Tull's Ian Anderson – they brought the deep-voiced Sam Galpin in on vocals and formed Mallard. They went on to record two albums for Virgin. Ironically – given the fact that one reason they split from Captain Beefheart was because of the music's simpler, more-commercial sound – they didn't go for a return to the adventurous, complex avant-garde style of the *Trout Mask Replica* era, nor the swampy blistering acid blues of *Clear Spot*. Their albums had a much softer country rock style that was almost as commercial as *Unconditionally Guaranteed*.

The question now has to be now asked, why the album was so bad. How could someone at the forefront of experimental avant-garde rock end up with such a bland, unadventurous, mainstream product? The answer is probably that Van Vliet was jealous, ambitious and resentful. He saw the success that Frank Zappa was enjoying with the Mothers. He also saw the success of many other bands he considered to be inferior and boring. He craved their recognition, fame and wealth. Don was a man who considered himself to be a genius, yet he was virtually unknown in his own country. Not content to remain an influential cult figure, he wanted success. He had hoped that simplifying the music on *The Spotlight Kid* and *Clear Spot* might've done the trick. But that compromise hadn't worked, and he decided he had to do something different.

Another element was that in late-1973, manager Grant Gibbs had been usurped by the DiMartino brothers. Andy and Auggie DiMartino were a pair of music-scene hustlers who were only in it for the money. They thought Beefheart would be a way for them to make an easy buck if they could only persuade him to become more commercial. They caught Don at the right moment, moved in and took over. Andy DiMartino not only managed Beefheart but acted as a roadie on the US tour, produced and even played on the album. (Incidentally, they also managed Buckwheat, from whom they recruited Dean Smith and sax player Del Simmons for the Tragic Band tour.) The two brothers were all over the operation. Under pressure from his new managers, Don became uncharacteristically quiescent, allowing them to take charge of his music, in the hopes they might come up with the goods. An indication of where Don's head was at the time, was that for once, he was sharing the writing credits with someone else: Andy DiMartino. Though probably for financial considerations, Don also included Jan, so Andy actually only received a third.

The title *Unconditionally Guaranteed* is a joke: guaranteed to be pretty tedious.

I'm not sure what Virgin Records thought of all this. After being eager to sign up the prestigious offbeat band, they now found themselves with two mediocre albums. Virgin later said that Beefheart albums not firing on full cylinders were still superior to those of most other bands. On reflection, I have to agree. Though they still stand as the nadir of Don's career, those two albums are not as bad as I thought they were at the time.

In hindsight, the album has some value with a number of reasonable tracks. But for those of us who grew up with Captain Beefheart's more ground-breaking revolutionary sound, this was a disappointing experience. We were used to complex polyrhythms, dissonance and powerful riffs, soaked with dense poetry writhing in surreal imagery. We craved exciting numbers that were right out on the edge. This contented easy-listening album was quite a departure and difficult to come to terms with. When I first heard it, I thought it was a complete sellout. I was shocked and dismayed.

Writing this book, I played this album for the first time in 47 years and can now appreciate the beauty of those soulful love songs, even though they're not the adventurous Beefheart that first blew me away. I can imagine that – in the right mood – I might even play this album again.

It was, perhaps, a dud. But as someone at Virgin said, there's no such thing as a totally bad Beefheart album.

'Upon the My-O-My' (Don Van Vliet, Jan Van Vliet, Andy DiMartino)

The album starts with what is probably its best track. The poem compares a relationship with a woman, to a ship tossed around by wind and waves, desperate hands trying to control her and a captain bellowing orders. Nature calls the shots, and the captain has no control against such a savage force.

As for the music, well, it's obviously an attempt to move the Beefheart oeuvre right into the middle of the road. The production is poor, orchestration dreadful, guitar sound thin and flute intonation awful, but amongst it, there are still snatches of great musicianship. While lacking quality control, the track has such potential that it could've been one of the greats had Ted Templeton been at the controls to help give it a real swampy blues feel. Sadly, the DiMartino production takes a lighter approach on what is Captain Beefheart's easy-listening album. Most of the good playing is submerged. The result is more like a submarine than a ship!

'Sugar Bowl. (Don Van Vliet, Jan Van Vliet, DiMartino)

Simple words, simple music. Is the sugar bowl used as a metaphor for the planet; for all of life, sex and evolution? You can take it any way you want. One suggestion is that the bowl's white powder originated in Bolivia. We only have one life, and the Captain is encouraging us to make the most of it: 'There's only one world, one sugar bowl'.

But the light production takes away any gravitas. It starts with a slow guitar and breaks into a jolly little number that feels more like a pop song than a Beefheart track: very light and conventional in structure. The strident guitars are hidden well down in the mix. Even the blues harp fails to add any weight. It's pleasant enough, but you don't listen to Beefheart for pleasant, do you? Zoot Horn Rollo said, 'Sugar Bowl is just an entire piece of shit... by far the worst thing I've ever played on'.

'New Electric Ride' (Don Van Vliet, Jan Van Vliet, DiMartino)

Beefheart takes us on a roller coaster ride. The planet is spinning and swerving through the stars as we make love under a heavenly blue sky: an idea that could've been further developed.

Musically it's just another gentle chugging track based on a simple repeating bass line. The guitars are nondescript, and except for one loud burst, are kept very much in the background. The guitar part is said to be a leftover from *Trout Mask Replica*, but you wouldn't know it. The band is lacklustre. It's another pleasant pop song of little consequence.

'Happy Love Song' (Don Van Vliet, Jan Van Vliet, DiMartino)

I can just imagine Andy DiMartino suggesting Don write a happy love song. That's what he did. There is some innuendo that could be taken a couple of ways, but it doesn't rescue the song from being a shallow ditty. The slow and soft guitars, unremarkable drums and bass line give it a pop sensibility. Even the sax sounds like a standard pop solo. The production, with uninspiring brass section, is boringly conventional and even the Captain's voice sounds raspy and bland. It makes for pleasant-enough background music, but nothing more. I can't actually believe that this is the same band that produced Decals.

'Magic Be' (Don Van Vliet, Jan Van Vliet, DiMartino)

This has 1960s beat guitars and simple drums and bass like we've gone back to 1965, except the 1965 band deployed a far greater range of experimentation and change. This is all too straightforward – a lullaby, just like other bands produced: the type of music that Don had so frequently castigated. He recites/ croons the lyric in a soft middle-of-the-road manner, reflecting a spiritual mood. He plays with words in a simple manner, with the premise that 'magic be' in everything. Unfortunately, the song is lacking in magic. It can be summed up as enjoyable, simple and unexceptional.

'Full Moon, Hot Sun' (Don Van Vliet, Jan Van Vliet, DiMartino)

Despite another standard format, this track at least has a lot of energy. I like it but as a Beefheart track? I don't know if it's the hot sun, but it has a Caribbean holiday feel to it; kinda jolly (I never thought I'd ever be describing a Beefheart number as jolly). The lyrics are simple but have a great repeating punchy hook. The girl might just find some loving under that hot sun.

'I Got Love on My Mind' (Don Van Vliet, Jan Van Vliet, DiMartino)

I'm enjoying this one, too, although it feels as if the whole underground avant- garde never happened. This has the structure and production of a mid-1960s British psychedelic pop number that could've been a hit from a band like The Yardbirds. The guitar leads into a great little song with a typical guitar solo, but nothing revolutionary or challenging about it. The track would've worked nicely in the A&M sessions. Even the lyrics have the bearing of a regular love song – the Captain is confused and conflicted; he doesn't know which girl to love: more like a teenager than a married man in his 30s.

The Captain is delving back to the pop side of his British R&B invasion roots in an attempt to become more commercial and gain wider appeal.

'This Is the Day' (Don Van Vliet, Jan Van Vliet, DiMartino)

Another contender for the best track on the album, It's a haunting love song, beautifully sung, with some amazing melodic guitar work from Zoot Horn Rollo. The organ intro leads to a simple three-chord progression with a pleasant melody. The voice is gentle and seductive, in another teenage dream about falling in love. Once again, the production is like a mid-1960s guitar- driven pop song.

Zoot slags this off, but though it lacks the complexity and challenge of Decals, the song is delightful. The result is a soulful track of great beauty.

'Lazy Music' (Don Van Vliet, Jan Van Vliet, DiMartino)

Contentment is not a word I'd usually associate with Beefheart. This song takes us to warm summer evenings, chilling out with a beer in hand and lying back under the stars. Don and his girl are looking out over the lake with the moon reflecting in the water whilst listening to relaxing romantic sounds.

Beautiful guitar and gentle harmonics capture the mood. Though the atmosphere is lost a little as the band builds, the soulful delivery carries it through. The lyric – more poetic than most on this album – evokes pleasant imagery: 'Where the moon shines in the water upside down/Where everything's slow like love'. Not the Beefheart we had come to love, but this new simpler style had its merits.

'Peaches' (Don Van Vliet, Jan Van Vliet, DiMartino)

The album ends with another throwback to the mid-1960s, a great repeating vocal, soulful delivery and pop production. I like the blues harp, which gives it more of an edge. This cheerful track has little content. The Captain has his eye on a juicy red-skin peach in another easy-listening song with an agreeable vocal delivery. It's pleasant enough, but there's nothing complex or sophisticated about it. It's totally lacking any experimental features. Give the man a peach.

Bluejeans & Moonbeams (1974)

Personnel:
Don Van Vliet 'Captain Beefheart': vocals, harmonica
Dean Smith: guitar, bottleneck guitar
Michael Smotherman: keyboards, backing vocals
Ty Grimes: percussion
Ira Ingber (Elliot Ingber's brother): bass
Bob West: bass on 'Observatory Crest'
Gene Pello: drums
Jimmy Caravan: keyboards, star machine
Mark Gibbons: keyboards
Personnel for 'Captain's Holiday': Chuck Blackwell: drums; Steve Hickerson: guitar; Richard Feldman: bass; Walt Richmond (of The Tractors): piano
Producer: Andy DiMartino
Engineer: Greg Ladanyi
Recorded at Stronghold Sound Recorders, Hollywood
Victor Haydon: cover painting
Des Strobel: art direction
Susanne Ayers: photography
Label: Virgin (UK), Mercury (USA)

Don was floundering. His band had acrimoniously deserted him and despite his pleadings, would not return. The last album – despite its mainstream pop production – received a few positive reviews amidst the slagging off, but made no commercial breakthrough. The fans slated the album and nicknamed the band The Tragic Band. The band disintegrated following the tour, leaving the Captain feeling abandoned again. He had nobody to transcribe his musical ideas, no arranger and no structure to hold onto. He must've been in a pretty dark place. However, as he was contractually bound, he set about producing another album for Virgin/Mercury. He persuaded drummer Ty Grimes and guitarist Dean Smith from the touring band to return. The rest had scarpered, so he had to use session musicians. Don was undeterred by criticism of the album's production as lightweight and foolishly retained producer Andy DiMartino. What could possibly go wrong?!

There weren't enough songs to complete the album. For the first time since the early albums, they recorded a cover song and a filler track that didn't even feature Captain Beefheart: hence the song's ironic title - 'Captain's Holiday'.

Engineer Greg Ladanyi (who went on to an illustrious career) was drafted in following the sacking of Al Thomas. At the time. Greg had absolutely no engineering experience and received hefty criticism for his work on the album. In his defence, he later said the band was tripping all the time (So much for Don's denial), and consequently, they were all over the place.

The budget wasn't sufficient and ran out before the album was completed. Given the situation, it was a wonder that any album was created at all. The verdict at the time was that the album was Beefheart's nadir, of no worth and an absolute disgrace. Beefheart later echoed this view, as did the ex-band members, who disowned it all together. I felt the same, but now I find myself enjoying the album despite its flaws and limitations. I think it was certainly an improvement on *Unconditionally Guaranteed*.

The album cover was painted by The Mascara Snake (Victor Hayden) and captures a weird acid vibe of a mystical Bambi leaping over a fence with strange electrified red blobs in the background. The cover also showed that Don no longer owned the band: they were now just The Magic Band.

In hindsight, this is a very bizarre album, but not in the normal Beefheartian sense. It's quite a mishmash of styles, with simple lyrics and orthodox music. It is much more listenable than I once thought. Some of the tracks are quite brilliant. Don sounds laid-back and content, like a man in love. He's not pushing the envelope and seems a little devoid of ideas. There is melody, beauty and tenderness, with a little blues and weirdness thrown in for good measure. It's not the best of albums but certainly has some high points.

'Party Of Special Things To Do' (Van Vliet, Elliot Ingber)
A slice of Beefheart humour opens the album. The comedy comes over well, and they get into a real swampy groove. The poetry is not as profound as on Trout, and the sound is less loaded with bluesy voodoo played on *Mirror Man* and *Clear Spot*. Beefheart is perhaps trying too hard to be Beefheart: weird for the sake of being weird. The poetry, music and song structure all sound forced; nothing flows naturally.

Following that 'camel in its nightie', we're off on an acid trip to somewhere darker than Alice's Wonderland. The 'Ace of Love' takes Don to the strange party. Looks like Greg Ladanyi was right: there was a lot of acid around. The acid-drenched lyrics and heavy ambience set the tone for a great adventure, and the Captain provides us with a vivid description. The track wades into the bayou with dangling Spanish moss and alligators. There are some great bluesy riffs and those opening guitars are like the duelling of old. Don uses his best howlin' Wolfman Jack voice to good effect. The lyrics take us back to *Mirror Man*, with Elixir Sue stepping out of her tarotplane along with the *Mirror Man*.

Despite being a powerful track, the Captain seems to have run out of fresh ideas, and is dredging up images and sounds from the past.

'Same Old Blues' (J. J. Cale)
Apart from adapting a few blues songs and performing some live covers, Don rarely played other people's work, but this is a worthy exception. Perhaps he was struggling to write new material. Nonetheless, he makes a great job of this J. J. Cale song. J. J. provided the classic blues tale: his woman has got another man, way across town. Don delivers the song in an orthodox blues style, racked with pain. He continues the first track's swampy feel with

classic chord sequences. His vocal delivery really suits this type of material. He howls in a high register before settling into a deep growl. J. J. created beauty, but Don makes it his own. Maybe he should've done more covers. He talked about doing an album of blues covers, but never managed to organise himself.

The band plays straight, without avant-garde embellishments. The strings add to the atmosphere, as do the two electric piano parts. Don frames the song with slices of blues harp. I do wonder what the first formation of the band with Doug Moon and Alex Snouffer would've made of this, as they were a masterful blues band – or what the later more inventive Zoot/Rockette/Winged Eel Fingerling/Drumbo combo would've done with the material.

After hearing those first two tracks, I was hoping that the whole album was going to be acid-tinged blues.

'Observatory Crest' (Van Vliet, Ingber)

When I first heard this, I was disappointed, but the track grew on me. From the first soft dreamy guitar, it's obvious that 'Observatory Crest' won't challenge the avant-garde, but it's a great slab of soul, which is another side to Don's creativity. Attuning my ear to this other facet of Beefheart always takes time. This track illustrates how he can be sentimental, nostalgic, and produce melodic offerings of soulful beauty.

Observatory Crest is at the Griffin Observatory in the hills overlooking Los Angeles. I've stood there many times, and the view – particularly at night – is incredible. Don visited the planetarium as a young boy.

Tripping after an L.A. concert, Don and his partner would drive out to the observatory, watch the stars spin and flying saucers whizz, in a delightfully stoned euphoria.

The music has a dreamy quality that reflects the spacey feel. There's not a hint of a hard sound. An easy flow with high-rising interstellar notes gently waft to caress the ears. Complex guitars interweave without a glimpse of a disparate rhythm or atonal signature; just a soft balmy melodic tone. The quality of the voice is calming, enabling us to feel the evening warmth, enjoyment and nostalgia. Don is bathing in the glow of a memory. It's totally beautiful and a complete contrast to his previous styles. No wonder the die-hard fans were appalled. This takes some getting used to, but we have caught glimpses of this style before, particularly on *Unconditionally Guaranteed*.

'Pompadour Swamp' (Don Van Vliet)

This was the original working title for the instrumental that became 'Suction Prints', but it isn't a great track. With a title like that, it should be more of a swampy blues. This production is too light and funky. The high pompadour hairstyle of the fifties had a swagger to it, but this production doesn't quite make it. All the ingredients are there but somehow lack the heavy bluster of the

Clear Spot production, which would have added that sleazy element. Shame. It could have been great.

What are we talking about here? Some fantastical nightclub? Some paradise with music? Who knows? I feel this track needed the *Clear Spot* treatment. The whole production is very linear and mainstream. The funky dance rhythm needs to be heavier. An opportunity lost.

'Captain's Holiday' (Richard Feldman, Walt Richmond, Stephen Hickerson, Chuck Blackwell)

This track is real filler. The title rather gives it away, as the track features neither the Captain nor any of the band members. It was included to make up the required number of tracks.

The whole album is on the light side, weighing in at just nine tracks. They needed more, but the Captain was out of material and ideas. The story goes that they found this track on a discarded tape. It's a bunch of Tulsa session men playing an excellent long instrumental that really captures a funky Tulsa sound. The Magic Band added some backing vocals and used it on the album. I'm not quite sure how they got away with it.

Having said that, I really like the track. The groove and guitar are infectious; it's just not at all like Beefheart!

'Rock 'n Roll's Evil Doll' (Van Vliet, Mark Gibbons, Ira Ingber)

This ventures into hard rock verging on heavy metal with this nightmarish song describing a bad trip in which a giant evil rock-chick sporting flashing eyes is rushing at him. It's a clichéd pastiche like something out of an Alice Cooper skit. I suspect Mark Gibbons and Winged Eel Fingerling's brother Ira had a lot to do with this track. It's not Don's style at all. It's a romp; a bad acid trip complete with hallucinations, rainbow halls and paranoia. It's much more conventional than we're used to.

'Further Than We've Gone' (Don Van Vliet)

This is positively schmaltzy, with melodic guitar, strings and soothing vocals, but is so laid-back it oozes syrup. The keyboards drip late-night-radio-love-song. The husky voice is imprisoned by a pedestrian backing and an arrangement that feels too light and jazzy. Even the extended guitar solo is innocuous. If someone had told me back in 1969 that Beefheart could produce a number like this, I wouldn't have believed them. He has jumped from the high board of cool into the pool of mainstream. It's too nice and harmless. You could listen to late-night radio on a summer evening and let this soothing track waft over you like a gentle massage.

Once I got over the shock and accepted this for what it was, I had to admit it was pretty good. It's just that words like 'gentle', 'soothing', 'schmaltzy', 'melodic' and 'pleasant' are not the type you'd normally associate with Beefheart. This man is a surprise. Versatility comes to mind!

'Twist Ah Luck' (Don Van Vliet, Mark Gibbons, Ira Ingber)

The title sounds like Beefheart, but the song is standard and mundane, with no hint of poetry. It's based on a guitar riff Keith Richards might've been proud of; remarkably Stones-ish. As well as riffs delivered in an orthodox rock format, there is a rambling bass line and harmonica in the background. This simpler, less-experimental format is certainly more accessible and commercial, but it lacks cutting edge. It's a great rock love song but a million miles from the complexity and mind-blowing adventure of vintage Beefheart.

This whole album poses a number of questions. Now that Beefheart lacked the time to train the musicians, and lacked a musical arranger to transmit his ideas, was he resigned to using a more mainstream style? Was the music inevitably simpler without the piano compositions? Were the musicians simply lacking in ability or too set in their ways to change to a more avant-garde style? This was a conscious effort by Beefheart, his manager and DiMartino simplify the music to create a more commercial sound. Was Don in a dark place; his experimental creative forces dried up? Had he lost his confidence? Or, as Greg suggested, were the musicians all simply too stoned to do anything else? Perhaps the music is the culmination of all that and more.

'Bluejeans & Moonbeams' (Van Vliet)

This is a unique track, and I can see why it titled the album as there is nothing quite like it. Right from that ethereal organ intro, we're into a different world. A contented Don is in relaxed mode gently crooning his love-drenched poetry. The vocal is clear and to the fore. The poetry – with all manner of wordplay – is sung over the top of a very quiet backing. The result is melodic, easy on the ear, and quite unlike anything he ever did before or after. The song has a spacey quality.

The slide guitar comes in at a very high pitch, with repeating ascending notes. The organ creates an underlying orchestral effect. An organ solo on a Beefheart track: daring or what? For me, it feels like Fleetwood Mac's 'Albatross' or even Procol Harum's 'A Whiter Shade Of Pale'.

Bongo Fury – Frank Zappa and The Mothers/Captain Beefheart (1975)

Personnel:
Frank Zappa: lead guitar (2, 5, 6, 9), backing vocals
Captain Beefheart: vocal, harp, soprano sax (1, 3, 4, 5, 8, 9,), backing vocals
George Duke: keyboards, vocals (2, 7), backing vocals
Napoleon Murphy Brock: sax, vocals (2, 7), backing vocals
Bruce Fowler: trombone
Tom Fowler: bass
Denny Walley: slide guitar, backing vocals
Terry Bozzio: drums
Chester Thompson: drums ('200 years old', 'Cucamonga')
Robert 'Frog' Camarena: backing vocals ('Debra Kadabra')
Recorded live at Armadillo World Headquarters, Texas; Record Plant, Los Angeles
Producer: Frank Zappa
Engineers: Michael Braunstein, Frank Hubach, Kelly Kotera, Davey Moire, Kerry McNabb, Mike Stone
Carl Schenkel: design
John Williams: photography
Label: DiscReet

Following the sojourn with Virgin and Mercury, there were legal shenanigans which prevented the release of any new material. Don was bereft of band, gigs and income. He needed help, and was forced to turn to his old friend Frank Zappa. After a fulsome apology from Don – as Frank stated: ('He apologised for all the garbagio and asked for a job') and putting aside their acrimonious differences following *Trout Mask Replica*, Frank agreed Don could join his band for a tour – for which Don sang, played harp, sax, and wrote a couple of songs. It was a collaboration of equals, though I can't quite see how that could possibly have worked for long given the egos of the two men.

Bongo Fury was recorded live, and overdubbed and mixed at the Record Plant in L.A, with three earlier studio recordings added ('200 Years Old Man', 'Cucamonga' and 'Muffin Man'). Frank and Don's relationship was often tense. Don dissociated himself from what was going on and tended to spend much time – even on stage – drawing in a large sketchpad. When he took centre stage he was determined to make his mark – throwing himself into the part with manic incantations that hung somewhere between beat poetry and electric preacher man.

With full-throttle vocals, he was not about to be upstaged by Frank. Don's performances inspired Frank to produce blistering guitar solos. This tour was the last outing for this incarnation of The Mothers and the first for drummer Terry Bozzio.

'Debra Kadabra' (Frank Zappa)

The album opens with Don's intense vocal: a hilarious melodramatic performance highlighting he and Frank's humour. It starts conventionally enough but following the guitar intro; everything rapidly mutates into one of Frank's zany creations. The song breaks into carefully choreographed sections of mad jazz and constipated voice as the Captain alternates his vocal with instrumental snatches, in an ever-increasing frenzy like a mad preacher on fire. The performance was designed to be visual.

Frank had a knack for introducing tempo variations, discordant outbursts, melodic phrases and intervals, mixing outrageously humorous lyrics with sections of normality. Nothing was ever straightforward. The track moves into an R&B section with Don exhorting and cajoling the witch Debra to take him with her.

He really launches himself into this theatrical production. He certainly seemed to enjoy this role, but it must've been hard for him to be part of Frank's carefully controlled piece. Like many of Frank's productions, this was tightly scripted theatre as much as musical composition. Don had to be well-rehearsed and master the timing (a novel experience for him), but this probably took some pressure off him. He certainly seemed to relish the role and was successful.

'Sam With The Showing Scalp Flat Top' (Don Van Vliet)

After a short horn intro, Don recites his surreal poetry, which paints many vivid images and teases the mind into finding rational meaning. The band emphasise the reading with noodling guitar and short bursts of sound. The piece builds in intensity, and near the end, Don's in full swing, roaring the 'bongo fury' lines that gave rise to the album title. The band adds to the intensity with a repetition of the 'Louie Louie' chords.

'Poofter's Froth Wyoming Plans Ahead' (Frank Zappa)

This piss-take is a send-up of redneck attitude and politics, unbridled capitalism and the resulting tacky consumerism. The lyric looks ahead to the USA's 200th anniversary and the way big business will incite patriotic fervour in order to sell a mass of plastic crap. There'll be 'doo-dads, flags, jackets, beer, pennants, little goods, paper cups': anything small and useless.

The music – a country and western pastiche – is suitably over the top. Frank was a brilliant writer of political satire. Behind the humour lies his complete disdain for shallow plastic culture, and how politicians and businessmen cynically use phoney patriotism in order to profit and gain votes.

Don is enjoying himself and delivers the song brilliantly. It was obviously a favourite of his, as he played it regularly on the 1975 UK and US Magic Band tours. The country and western style is different to anything he sang before or after. Even the harmonica playing with little comical send-ups is unique.

'Advance Romance' (Frank Zappa)

Don's minor role here was to add great harmonica phrases and a few asides to Zappa's sleazy tale. A sexy woman took an unfortunate guy for a ride, and he ended up fleeced: 'She's taken it all and locked him out'. She was a serial lover on the make. He warned his best friend Potato-headed Bobby, saying she was the Devil, but Bobby thought he'd try her out anyway. He popped 'round and had his 'fry frenched'. 'She's from Utah, you know'. Frank had the rare talent for injecting humour into any situation. This 'romance' certainly 'advanced' into a farce.

Jazz fragments break up this bluesy number. The tightly-choreographed piece has searing guitar breaks and snatches of instruments that burst out in a seemingly random way, but nothing was ever random in a Zappa production. The song finally settles into an extended guitar jam with fabulous bass and occasional interjections from other instruments. Frank's musicians were all top-drawer and well-rehearsed.

'Man With The Woman Head' (Don Van Vliet)

Another of Don's surreal beat poems clearly recited over The Mothers' quiet jazz backing. It's a detailed description of Ace – an ancient opium addict who has bony nicotine-stained fingers, a thin skull-like face, dark circles around the eyes, chipped yellow wooden teeth, grey suit, straw loafers and a truculent manner. William Burroughs comes to mind.

Not only did Frank give Don a job on the road and equal billing on the *Bongo Fury* album, he also included Don on Frank Zappa And The Mothers Of Invention's 1975 album *One Size Fits All* (playing the harmonica under the pseudonym Bloodshot Rollin' Red), and 1976's *Zoot Allures*, where Don plays harmonica on 'Find Her Finer'.

A live vocal contribution of 'The Torture Never Stops' appears on the Zappa albums You Can't Do That On Stage Anymore Vol. 4 and Cheap Thrills.

Bat Chain Puller (1975 – released 2012)

Personnel:
Don Van Vliet 'Captain Beefheart': vocals, harmonica, soprano sax
John French 'Drumbo': drums, guitar
Jeff 'Morris' Tepper: guitar
Denny 'Feelers Rebo' Walley: guitar
John Thomas: piano, electric piano, Moog synthesizer, bass, effects
Recorded at Paramount Studio, L.A.
Producers: Don Van Vliet, Kerry McNabb
Arranger: John 'Drumbo' French
Don Van Vliet: painting
Gail Zappa: art direction, photography
Michael Mesker: graphics, photography

After returning from the *Bongo Fury* tour, Don was energised. He had new material and was offered the chance to record for Frank Zappa's DiscReet label. Having learnt his lesson with *Trout Mask Replica*, Frank was not directly involved but still offered Don generous studio time.

Don immediately set about putting together a new band. John 'Drumbo' French was back in the fold as drummer, an unlikely guitarist, and more importantly, as music arranger. This proved to be crucial, as Don now had someone with whom he could share his musical vision, to transcribe ideas and organise the band to deliver them: something that was severely lacking on the previous two albums. He also brought in Jeff Tepper: a guy he'd met when studying art. Jeff had a unique guitar style. Denny 'Feelers Rebo' Walley was poached from The Mothers, and John Thomas – a friend of John 'Drumbo' French (who had played alongside him in the band Rattlesnake & Eggs, and the early incarnation of Mallard) – was recruited on bass and Moog synthesiser.

Entering Paramount Studio, recording proceeded well. Unbeknownst to them, the sessions were being financed by Frank Zappa's business partner Herb Cohen, using Frank's royalty money. Frank was not aware of this use of his money, nor of a number of other financial transactions that Herb was involved in. This all ended in a big falling out and the termination of their business partnership.

Copies of the resulting tapes were sent to Virgin Records, who were keen to put the album out. But Zappa and Cohen's legal wrangling made this difficult. They both demanded that Virgin pay them an advance. The financial situation became messy. Zappa withheld the tapes, and Cohen sued Zappa. Don was caught in the middle and couldn't release the album. The tapes sat on the shelf until 2012 and were finally released after Don's death.

In the meantime, Don re-recorded a number of the songs for the 1978 Warner Bros. album *Shiny Beast (Bat Chain Puller)*. Other songs were re-recorded for 1980's *Doc at the Radar Station* and 1982's *Ice Cream For Crow*.

In a further twist to the story, Don was recording *Ice Cream for Crow* when Zappa and Cohen's legal dispute was finally resolved. Now that the recordings were available, Don wanted to use a number of unreleased tracks from the original *Bat Chain Puller* to complete Ice Cream For Crow. He went to Frank for permission, but they had an unpleasant row and Frank refused. Don had to re-record them.

Much later, there was talk of releasing *Bat Chain Puller* in its original form, but this time – probably because he'd re-recorded most of the tracks – Don was opposed to doing so. Eventually, Gail Zappa – who was managing the estate of her deceased husband Frank – decided to issue them, with three bonus tracks, in 2012. The recordings were remastered by John French and Denny Walley and featured artwork by Don.

As the tapes sent to Virgin Records in 1976 had been prematurely circulated to a number of radio stations, they were widely bootlegged. I have a few different versions, so I was familiar with the album before it was released and loved the new songs, however, I was pleased to find that the official CD (2012) was so much brighter and clearer than any of those bootlegs.

For those who had not heard the bootlegs, initial expectations were low. With the disappointment of the previous two albums, the opinion was that Beefheart's creative energies had deserted him and he'd lapsed into a commercial quagmire.

But *Bat Chain Puller* felt like a rebirth: the Captain was firing on all cylinders again. Free of the DiMartino brothers' insidious commercial influence, the album was packed with innovation, invention and variety. Beefheart was back! If only it had seen the light of day in 1976, it might've given Don's career fresh impetus, led to more touring and kept that band together: including Denny Walley, who was superb and a major loss. But that was not to be, and we had to wait until 1978 for the next recordings and yet another incarnation of the Magic Band. Two years sadly lost!

'Bat Chain Puller' (Don Vliet)

Right from the opening thudding drum rhythm with oscillating harmonica and guitar, we know we're in for something great!! Don's back! Having shaken off the shackles of the DiMartino brothers, he was free to express himself. It shows!! Power and confidence shriek boastfully from his delivery.

The rhythm is based on Don's windscreen wipers, which he recorded and played to the band. The bass and two guitars set up interweaving riffs and harsh patterns, synchronising, intermeshing, falling apart as the steady, authoritative rhythm and bass hold the track on course. Like a monster released from its cage, Don unleashes a vocal that's rich and uncompromising. This is the real thing: music like no other.

The track has the quality of a gothic horror film – unique, with weird chirping guitar noises, unearthly bats, or the sound of a chainsaw. The piece is dense, and the howlin' voice – full of nuance, expression and sheer force – delivers one of Don's most inventive songs. The poetry – back to his surreal best – is layered with otherworldly imagery straight from Don's brain; his grey tubes 'containing all his thoughts and belongings', on the theme of the destruction of the environment.

What with 'marshmallow soot' and 'green Sashes drawn by rubber dolphins with gold yawning mouths that blister and break in agony/In zones of rust', we're lost in a Dali-esque landscape where a simple bell-pull/chainsaw puller is transformed into an alien artefact in a soundscape that could've been born on another planet. Bliss! This was re-recorded for *Shiny Beast (Bat Chain Puller)*.

'Seam Crooked Sam' (Don Vliet)

Interestingly, John French is on guitar. He sure is versatile and talented. This is a different texture and harks back to *Trout Mask Replica*. Synchronised guitar and keyboard pick out the melody with a sparse bass, all dancing with each other. With that same swagger and bravado, Don recites this opaque poem, bringing it to life with vivid imagery. This is the tale of Seam Crooked Sam: a strange, eccentric character. Where are we? I could be wrong, but I get the impression of some wild-west frontier town – a brothel/bar/general store, sawdust on the floor, dancing and wildness; dinner's ready, apple pie on the table! I'm reminded of Jack Kerouac's recorded poetry as the backing becomes jazz-like. The guitars and keyboard intermingle and meander, with bass interjecting. Fabulous. This was never re-recorded or officially released elsewhere.

'Harry Irene' (Don Vliet)

Now for something completely different. I wasn't sure about this. At first, it sounded like a return to the conventional. It tells the story of a couple who ran a canteen together, serving tuna sandwiches to die for. Unusual for the 1970s, they were a lesbian/transvestite couple. Life was great until Irene left with Dusty and all the 'readies'.

The music is linear and drum-led. The bass emphasises, setting up a strong swaying swing rhythm, embellished with accordion, keyboard and a later whistling section. Don's voice is relaxed, almost crooning, melodic and rich. It sounds very Gallic.

This was re-recorded for *Shiny Beast (Bat Chain Puller)*.

'81 Poop Hatch' (Don Vliet)

A straightforward poem recitation. Like most of his poetry, the essence is clear, even if the meaning is not. It's full of minutely-detailed observation. Don is sitting in some wasteland by a lily pond, reading a book a friend has given him. Visions from the book mingle with everything around him. An old car rusts on an overgrown area:

Wire and wood
Tires, bottles and the berries

Heat swims on its fenders
Mice played in air holes and valves

In the distance is the sound of poor families laughing and starving babies crying as irritating banal pop music plays. 'He has to go off to pick up his horns/But his head won't move until it walks'. It's all very strange as if fragments of a dream. This was re-recorded for *Ice Cream For Crow*.

'Flavor Bud Living' (Don Vliet)

This features more guitar-playing from John 'Drumbo' French. The piece is a short melodic guitar solo. It sounds as if written on piano, but with fewer notes, it's slower, more fluid and less spiky than Don's usual piano compositions. This was re-recorded for Doc at the Radar Station.

'Brick Bats' (Don Vliet)

This is the album's most raucous number. I think the good old Captain has received more than his fair share of brickbats from critics, but these brickbats are real. They are alive, being fried up his chimney. We're back to the dissonance typified by squealing horns and atonal phrases, an anguished vocal and changes of tempo and rhythm. It's a track that would not have been out of place on *Trout Mask Replica*.

This shrieks to me of a bad trip with those poor creatures burning up in the fire, his mind becoming a bat, threatening to dash its brains out before regathering itself to 'make the evening more interesting'. The drawn-out ending of the hoarse and anguished repeated 'Brick bats' to a lurching rhythm, crashing cymbals and screeching horns completes a unique song. It's classic Beefheart that would entice a few more brickbats from bemused critics. This was re-recorded for Doc at the Radar Station.

'Floppy Boot Stomp' (Don Vliet)

This track is up there with the best that Beefheart has produced. What an incendiary song. I always saw this as a poem about the Third World War: 'The night turned white in the middle of the night' perhaps being a nuclear explosion. On a more symbolic level, it's a classic tale of the battle between good and evil. The old farmer takes on the Devil, the circle is drawn and the Devil steps in. The song erupts into a maelstrom as they compete in a fearsome dance, ending with the farmer pulling the Devil's horns off and fiddlin' him down the road. 'The hot lick kicked, and the fire leaped an' licked'. And there sure are some hot licks in there as that farmer has his square-dancing 'hoodoo hoedown' with the Devil. Hot stuff.

Starting with slide guitar busting in, second guitar riffing, drum and bass setting a fast tempo, the voice booms in low register – better than ever, full of confidence and authority. There are times when Don pushes the accelerator down, giving vent to the full force of his vocal cords. The intensity builds and diminishes with ominous riffs, a storming chorus and backing vocals. It's got everything: high-pitched guitar, sliding descents, and synchronised riffs in different tones. This was re-recorded for *Shiny Beast (Bat Chain Puller)*.

'Ah Carrot Is As Close As Ah Rabbit Gets To A Diamond' (Don Vliet)

A short keyboard instrumental with a haunting melody containing some forceful heavy-handed notes, followed by a softer section. This was re-recorded for Doc at the Radar Station.

'Owed T' Alex' (Don Vliet, Herb Bermann)

Herb Bermann wrote this poem, which could've been included on the first album in 1967, but perhaps was never properly recorded and certainly was never released. This 1975 version is probably quite different to that early version, but we'll never know. The song was originally called 'Carson City'. The Alex in question is Alex St. Clair Snouffer: a member of that original band. It's about a motorbike accident in Carson City. What Alex has to do with that, is unclear. The central character leaves home with a motorcycle gang (complete with iron crosses, helmets and patches), in search of love and parties, before taking a near-fatal spill. Was that Alex?

The placid riffs develop and the band really lets loose, with Don's strong vocal becoming more intense. The swaying rhythm gets you jigging.

This was re-recorded for *Shiny Beast (Bat Chain Puller)*.

'Odd Jobs' (Don Vliet)

I don't know why this was never used or re-recorded for any future album. It's a sublime song/poem, with an exquisite vocal delivery. Don recites the first verse, then takes to singing it over the top of the band, in a repeating cycle. The music is steady, with edgy, striking chords, maintained through an extended outro that's almost long enough to be an instrumental in its own right. That's John 'Drumbo' French on guitar again!

As for the poem, who was this odd-job man that the girls and women were all crazy over? He was a guy who came around on his rusty old bike and gave out candy. Is Don implying some drug dealing? Sounds like everything has been neglected since the guy disappeared, with 'Spider webs on the windows, dead flies and peeling linoleum': even 'the door knob's off'. Do they miss his handiwork or something more? It's okay, here he comes again: 'A bag of skin 'n' bones' on his old bike.

This was never re-recorded or officially released elsewhere.

'Human Totem Pole (The 1000th And 10th Day Of The Human Totem Pole)' (Don Vliet)

Here Don recites a poem full of tantalising images of a totem pole made of living human beings, 'Eyes rolling, ears wiggling, hands waving as they seek balance whilst performing their isometric exercises, chattering unhappily, and shitting on the ones below'. What is this about? The Statue of Liberty? Life in skyscrapers? Native American totem poles? A metaphor for the human condition or the inequality of mankind? Who knows what went on in Don's mind.

His delivery is clear and bright, full of suppressed humour. We're in the realm of vintage Beefheart again, with the guitars finishing each other's lines, the music pausing and restarting. Original and brilliant in every respect.

This was re-recorded for *Ice Cream for Crow*.

'Apes-Ma' (Don Vliet)

An ape inspired this in the Observatory Heights zoo that Don used to visit as a boy. It's a poem minus instrumental backing, full of empathy and pathos, not so much recited as performed. It's ostensibly the story of an ageing ape stuck in a cage that's too small, having lost the will to break out. She has nothing to do but eat and shit and is now so old that the little girl who named her Apes Ma, has died.

The version later released on *Shiny Beast (Bat Chain Puller)* sounds exactly the same.

Bonus Track
'Bat Chain Puller' (Alternative mix) (Don Vliet)

This version was mixed by Kerry McNabb. It sounds a little busier, with more bass, but is not significantly different. I'm happy with either!

'Candle Mambo' (Don Vliet)

This track was mixed by Spence Chrislu. It's a romantic love song. Don describes dancing in the moonlight with his love, to the flickering of a candle. He's playing with words in much the same way that he did with 'Gimme That Harp Boy', except now he's applying wordplay to a candle. He starts in his best pirate voice – 'Avast me hearties' – before the intro begins. Plenty of duelling follows, but as the track progresses, the music becomes more melodic. The outro has some of John French's great drum patterns.

Though the music is dynamic, the lyric is saccharin-sweet and somewhat incongruous with the Captain's persona. I find it hard to imagine him doing everyday chores; even harder imagining him dancing romantically in a candlelit room. If I do visualise this scene, I see him in a stovepipe hat and longtail coat! Zoot says Don puts on a Beefheart guise when in public, but in private life is just an ordinary guy who is capable of being romantic.

This was re-recorded for *Shiny Beast (Bat Chain Puller)*.

'Hobo-ism' (Don Vliet, Denny Walley)

This is the pick of the bonus tracks. It's over eight minutes long and was viewed as a possible single, but never released. The demo emerged from an impromptu session recorded on portable equipment, much in the way 'China

Pig' had been recorded for *Trout Mask Replica*. Denny Wally spontaneously created the music for this (a punchy delta blues on acoustic guitar) while Don wrote the lyrics and played vocal and harmonica.

Unfortunately, this is a substandard take recorded after drinking a bottle of tequila. Denny's playing is inferior, and Don mangles the lyric in a couple of places, so I don't know why they used this take. A better version was widely bootlegged and later released as a download on the ITunes *Bat Chain Puller* release.

It's a railroad song about a hobo riding the blinds. After stabbing his wife, he's on the run, cold, drunk and hungry, but he's free: free to bum rides, bum food and drink. It's the philosophy of the hobo. 'It's not that, not this, 'n' its hobo-ism/Not jazz, not jizzum, it's railroad-ism'.

The rhythm of a train saturates the playing. The words sound improvised, but they probably weren't. On the inferior take, Denny's acoustic playing breaks up in a couple of places, and Don sounds worse for wear, sometimes mumbling and stumbling. Nonetheless, even this version is fabulous.

This was never re-recorded and was only officially released on ITunes.

Shiny Beast (Bat Chain Puller) (1978)

Personnel:
Don Van Vliet 'Captain Beefheart': vocals, harmonica, soprano sax, whistling
Jeff 'Moris' Tepper: slide guitar, guitar
Richard Redus: slide guitar, bottleneck guitar, guitar, accordion, fretless bass
Artie Tripp 'Ed Marimba': marimba, percussion
Robert Arthur Williams: drums, percussion
Eric Drew Feldman: synthesizer, Rhodes piano, grand piano, bass
Bruce Lambourne Fowler: trombone, air bass
Recorded at The Automatt, San Francisco
Producers: Don Van Vliet, Pete Johnson
Label: Warner Bros.

With John 'Drumbo' French, Denny 'Feelers Rebo' Walley and John Thomas all leaving, there were again changes to the lineup. The new musicians were good but lacked the vitality and innovative skills of previous bands. Zoot Horn Rollo and Feelers Rebo were sadly missed. Even so, the band produced an album that was considerably better than either of the two Virgin albums, and Bruce Fowler's trombone-playing added a new dimension.

While the album was released in 1978 in the USA, it was not released in the UK until 1980. Fortunately, I was teaching in Los Angeles during 1979/1980, and bought a copy a year before any of my mates. During that year in the States, I travelled extensively during school holidays. I delivered a slide presentation of places I'd been, with an accompaniment of music from my newly acquired *Shiny Beast (Bat Chain Puller)*. Some really enjoyed it, but a number of my 17-year-old students hated the music, and one even said, 'Can't we just look at the slides without the ghastly music?'. I laughed and delighted in shocking them with a bit of Beef!

Don was short on inspiration. He included five re-recordings of *Bat Chain Puller* songs: 'Floppy Boot Stomp', 'Bat Chain Puller', 'Harry Irene', 'Owed T' Alex', and the outtake 'Candle Mambo'. As the original tapes were still subject to legal proceedings, the re-recordings were necessary.

Don also revised some unreleased older songs – 'Big Black Baby Shoes' became 'Ice Rose', and a *Clear Spot* outtake titled 'Pompadour Swamp' (totally different to the track on 1974's *Bluejeans & Moonbeams*) became 'Suction Prints'. 'Apes-Ma' – recorded on Don's home recorder for *Bat Chain Puller* – was able to be used as it was. That meant that there were really only four new compositions, and one of those – 'Tropical Hot Dog Night' – was based on the 'Odd Jobs' riff. Don had not had a very productive two years!

Other new songs attempted in the sessions, didn't work. These included 'Drink Paint Run Run' and 'The Witch Doctor Life'. The former was modified and re-recorded for *Doc at the Radar Station* (becoming 'Run Paint Run Run'), and the latter was re-recorded for Ice Cream For Crow.

Most saw *Shiny Beast (Bat Chain Puller)* as a big leap forward from the two Virgin/Mercury albums. Many of the elements that had attracted us to the Captain in the first place, were back: driving music, clashing guitars, searing notes, innovation, experimentation and spoken word. All we'd heard of *Bat Chain Puller* were bootlegs. Now, with a proper version, we are in a position to make comparisons. Back then, we just thought Shiny Beast was great.

Looking back at *Shiny Beast (Bat Chain Puller)*, I can see it from a better perspective, and as a great step forward. It was perhaps not as bright as the original *Bat Chain Puller*, but it remains one of Don's major works.

'The Floppy Boot Stomp' (Van Vliet)
A faithful re-recording of the *Bat Chain Puller* song. This came out slightly shorter, and sounds constrained. I prefer the earlier version, but this is good.

'Tropical Hot Dog Night' (Van Vliet)
On the surface this has a positive Caribbean carnival sound, with chirpy bright West Indian music lighting up the barbeque with a catchy hook and melody. Underneath, it's something else. The words have that surreal Beefheart quality: 'Two flamingos in a fruit fight'. This is an acid BBQ. 'Every colour of day whirlin' 'round at night'. The Captain's looking to party. That's where the song becomes dark. The 'young girls' may just 'meet that monster tonight'.

The music is layered and more complex than the first hearing of the bright sound might suggest.

Following the release of her early albums, PJ Harvey was in contact with Don, and reputedly spent hours in long phone conversations with him right up until his death. He was a big fan of her work. She produced a song called 'Meet Ze Monsta' in 2004 that was a response to this song.

This is what Polly said about Don in the preface in the catalogue for Don Van Vliet's art exhibtion at the Anton Kern Gallery in New York in 2007 - 'I feel very fortunate in my life, for many reasons. One of these reasons is coming across such a man as Don Van Vliet, through his music, his art and as a friend'.

'Ice Rose' (Van Vliet)
This riff had its origins in an outtake from the first album, called 'Big Black Baby Shoes'. That earlier track had a much heavier feel with Alex St. Clair Snouffer playing a mean slide guitar. 'Ice Rose' is more textured, the marimba creating a much lighter feel. Instead of slide guitar, trombone leads the piece.

It's strange but also melodic. At times it's like there are two different tunes going at the same time, but not really relating to each other. The changes in tempo are very Zappa-ish.

'Harry Irene' (Van Vliet)
Harry Irene is another re-recording of a *Bat Chain Puller* song. The brushed drums are like annoying interference to me. The track is muffled and subdued

compared to the original: not that I noticed that before hearing the original Bat Chain Puller.

'You Know You're A Man' (Van Vliet)

This is not one of my favourites. It's a love song with a difference. It has its moments – like a snazzy guitar solo – but is ultimately lightweight. Don performs some vocal gymnastics, but even so, the track just plods along. The lyrics are banal: 'I know I'm a man/You know you're a girl'. That might be fine if the Captain had built on it and taken it somewhere. The lyrics feel as if he was struggling for ideas. It lacks any textured poetry. That, coupled with the lack of musical innovation or thrust leaves the end product weak.

Don had been forced to resurrect old ideas. The new ideas – even the fabulous 'Drink Paint, Run Run' and 'The Witch Doctor Life' (later successfully re-recorded) – weren't working and had to be abandoned. 'You Know You're A Man' is symptomatic of his general malaise, and feels pedestrian.

'Bat Chain Puller' (Van Vliet)

Another re-recording from Bat Chain Puller. I love both versions, but the original has more punch and power.

'When I See Mommy I Feel Like A Mummy' (Van Vliet)

This is the best of the new compositions – extraordinarily inventive, complex and experimental, new and wonderful. The varied components work. The lyrics venture into new thought-provoking territory.

It's clear from the beginning that the trombone is the star of the song. Two guitars weave together wonderfully, the drum rhythms are fantastic and mirrored by the trombone. The bass is perfect, again emphasising the rhythm and melody. Complex changing rhythms, novel instrumentation and repeated guitar phrases all work together exquisitely, like nothing I'd ever heard before. I'm not usually a fan of choruses, but this one works brilliantly. The vocal is precise and expressive.

Even the lyrics are innovative. Don – an only child and thought to be an artistic child prodigy – was incredibly indulged by his mother, who he called Sue. Their relationship was very close but verged on abusive. He treated her as a servant, demanding she bring him food and Pepsi. After his father suffered a heart attack, Don had to leave school and start work. He worked delivering bread, and as a shoe salesman and vacuum cleaner salesman to help support the extended family. Don's relationship with his mother continued to be complex and deep. He'd built up an exaggerated image of himself as Captain Beefheart, but that was at odds with how he was at home. The real Don (kept hidden from the outside world) could be himself with his mother. The poem captures the claustrophobic effect that a mother can impose on her sons. To her, they will always be children. Then there's the son's view of his mother and his difficulty in seeing her as a human being outside her role as a mother.

'Owed T'Alex' (Van Vliet, Herb Bermann)
Personally, I still prefer the original *Bat Chain Puller* version. Though this is a rockier version, it has more instrumentation in the production and a peculiar squeaky harmonica sound. The original version was pared back and sharper, with a cleaner, brighter feel.

'Candle Mambo' (Van Vliet)
This is a totally different production to the original *Bat Chain Puller* outtake. This marimba version with horns doesn't have the same impact as the guitar version.

'Love Lies' (Van Vliet)
This is very different to anything the Captain had done before. With marimba, guitar, trombone and bass, the musicians create a gentle lazy rhythm that sits within a more orthodox structure; the instruments combine to fashion a complex composition. The emotion-laden voice melds with the music to craft something hauntingly beautiful, wistful and utterly delightful.

The lyric admirably captures the tale of a lovelorn guy sitting in his car outside his girlfriend's house. Full of regret, the tears in his eyes make the streetlights 'flutter like fireflies'. She's out with another guy.

'Suction Prints' (Van Vliet)
This instrumental started life as the *Clear Spot* outtake 'Pompadour Swamp'. It was nothing to do with the song on *Bluejeans & Moonbeams*: only the title was taken from that. It's an exciting number that's very different to its earlier incarnation and was nearly always used to open their stage act.

'Pompadour Swamp' (not included on *Clear Spot*) featured fluent guitar with bubbling bass, a second guitar playing riffs in counterpoint, and intermittent drums; music building in intensity, dropping out, warbling high slide notes, spaces and tempo variation. This version is a different species. It's much fuller and faster with a bigger sound. There's less space, great slide guitar, more drums and bass and a squealing atonal horn part. The trombone really alters the texture, making it fuller. The faster rhythms near the end are very Zappa-ish; shades of 'The Blimp' without the intervals.

'Apes-Ma' (Van Vliet)
This is the same recording from *Bat Chain Puller*. Don recorded it himself on his home recording machine, so he was able to use it as it was.

Blue Collar Soundtrack
In 1978, Don was asked to sing on a track written by Ry Cooder, Jack Nitzsche and Paul Schrader, for the film *Blue Collar*, produced by Paul Schrader. Recorded for MCA, the song was called 'Hard Workin' Man'. The film version was obscene, but a second, cleaner version was recorded in the hope that

it might obtain radio coverage. The cleaned-up track was released on the
soundtrack album and as a single. The B-side was a Jack Nitzsche number
called 'Coke Machine', that didn't include Don.

'Hard Workin' Man' (Cooder, Nitzsche, Schrader)
The song starts with a slow rhythmic industrial hammering, and proceeds with
a heavy chord structure into an arrangement of the Muddy Waters/Willie Dixon/
Bo Diddley song 'Mannish Boy' ('I'm A Man'). Ry Cooder played guitar on this.
Despite their past history, he actually recommended Don for the vocal. The
obscene movie version appears on the 1994 rarities compilation If You Got Ears.

The song has a standard blues format, with searing guitar. It's about a hard
hammer-wielding working man. Don delivers it in his best blues manner. His
deep resonant voice is perfect for the track.

Doc at the Radar Station (1980)

Personnel:

Don Van Vliet 'Captain Beefheart': vocals, Chinese gongs, harmonica, soprano sax, bass clarinet

John 'Drumbo' French: slide guitar, guitar, bass, drums ('Ashtray Heart', 'Sheriff Of Hong Kong'), marimba ('Making Love To A Vampire With A Monkey On My Knee'), vocals ('Dirty Blue Gene', 'Run Paint Run Run')

Jeff 'Moris' Tepper: slide guitar, guitar, nerve guitar, vocals ('Run Paint Run Run')

Eric Drew Feldman: synthesizer, bass, mellotron, grand piano, electric piano, vocals ('Run Paint Run Run')

Robert Arthur Williams: drums, vocals ('Run Paint Run Run')

Gary 'Mantis' Lucas: guitar ('Flavor Bud Living', French horn ('Best Batch Yet')

Bruce Lambourne Fowler: trombone ('Run Paint Run Run')

Studio: Sound Castle, Los Angeles

Producer: Don Van Vliet

Engineers: Glen Kolotkin, Mitchell Gibson

Don Van Vliet: cover painting and drawings

Michael Hollyfield: art direction and design

Michael Kent Rothman: photography

Label: Virgin

If *Shiny Beast (Bat Chain Puller)* was the trailer for a Beefheart resurgence, *Doc at the Radar Station* was the real thing. Getting John 'Drumbo' French back into the fold was perhaps the crucial element.

But despite the album's brilliance, the Captain was still devoid of new ideas. Three of the tracks – 'A Carrot Is as Close As A Rabbit Gets To A Diamond', 'Flavor Bud Living' and 'Brickbats' – were re-recordings of *Bat Chain Puller* songs. 'Run Paint Run Run' and 'The Witch Doctor Life' were Shiny Beast outtakes that Don reworked. The bulk of the remaining tracks were developed from fragments and ideas from the vault. Surprisingly, the end result was superb and back to the level of his blistering best, full of invention, variety and brilliant musicianship. The album surely rates right up there with Trout and Decals.

Doc at the Radar Station may have been constructed from past fragments and re-recordings, but it has ended up as a real tour de force. There's not a dud on it, and the Captain is firing at his creative finest. One of the best!

'Hot Head' (Van Vliet)

From the moment the guitar kicks in with that dirty riff, you know you're in for a storm. The band whip up a Louisiana hurricane. The drums and bass thud through your body, and Don's voice is at its snarling best. The repeating riff gets you rockin' and is wickedly visceral. The lead guitars intersperse piercing runs and searing notes with bursts of organ and even a little backing vocal. The bass picks up the riff, the rhythms intertwine and the rhythms pound in your brain. It's disturbingly addictive. 'She's a wild creature, a hot head/So full of life she'll tear you up', 'She'll burn you up in bed/She'll drive you mad'.

'Ashtray Heart' (Van Vliet)
This slams into you with drums, bass and another filthy riff. The band play complex rhythms with searing slide guitars. The anguished voice is full of accusation. His heart has been used like an ashtray.

Don's back to his most surreal lyrics: 'I feel like a glass shrimp in a pink panty with a saccharine chaperone', 'Somebody's had too much to think', 'Open up another case of the punks'. His voice is aching with righteous fury. During the organ interlude, he recites poetry, before the band thuds back in with a crazy riff that's hypnotically pounding and hammers at your guts. There's so much going on – intricate instrumentation with tempo variations and Don's emotional drawling vocal. The abrupt end leaves everything hanging.

'A Carrot Is as Close as A Rabbit Gets To A Diamond' (Van Vliet)
Originally recorded for *Bat Chain Puller* but re-recorded here. There is a pastoral feel (a sharp contrast to tracks 1 and 2); a note-for-note rendition of the original, but with a different vibe. This version is softer, which accentuates the haunting melody. But the recording is less vibrant than the original.

'Run Paint Run Run' (Van Vliet)
This track was attempted at the Shiny Beast sessions as 'Drink Paint Run Run', but didn't make the grade. But it certainly makes the grade here, as Don develops the ideas further.

This showcase for his humour starts in a jaunty shuffling rhythm. The slide guitar picks up the refrain, and the chorus (exhorting the paint to run!) punctuates the song. I bet the band had great fun recording this. The trombone embellishes the track and there's even the return of a dash of theremin.

Don is probably alluding to his artwork in this song, with more play-on-words. He's made the paint into a character. Is it in a race, or fleeing from something sinister? 'Run paint, run run!'

'Sue Egypt' (Van Vliet)
These images conjure a splash of voodoo, hexes and spells and a wizard kiss. We're on a boat to forever, creeping through the ether on a mystical journey through life, through reality, or at least the smoky illusion of reality. Sue Egypt – a sorceress – is guiding us through the ancient Egyptian rituals of death, across the river into the lands beyond. Don's mother's name was Sue, and Egypt is where mummies come from. Don is venturing into 'When I See Mommy I Feel Like A Mummy' territory. He recites his opaque poetry over the top of loud and discordant guitar riffs. A simple bass line moves underneath, with flute interjections. The organ chords create a sinister feel.

'Brickbats' (Van Vliet)

Another track originally recorded for *Bat Chain Puller* and re-recorded here. This version is nowhere near as raucous. The horns are fewer and further back in the mix, making the track less chaotic, easier on the ear, and so creating a very different feel.

The intervening five years had probably lessened the nightmare experience of that bad acid trip, but we are still presented with two minutes and 40 seconds of a man greatly in need of help! It's a very disturbing poem, linking bats roasting in the fire – squeaking and flexing their little claws – with brickbats (as in, criticism), and brickbats as pieces of brick used as missiles. It's a powerful composition.

'Dirty Blue Gene' (Van Vliet)

This started life as an instrumental outtake from the *Safe as Milk* sessions, though I personally can't distinguish any relationship between the two.

This is wild. It starts with a madly strummed guitar, and takes off into a magnetic storm of sound, with Don sounding distraught, picked guitars, clashing riffs, weird slides, raging drums and changing tempos.

'If you've got ears, you gotta listen' to this aural lesson on genetics, straight out of that 'shiny beast of thought' housed in our heads. It's a tale of sex, attraction, infidelity and lust. Selfish genes lead us to sexual indiscretions, seeking the variety and mixing of genetic material. 'She's not bad, she's genetically mean'. Schizophrenically, there are two Dons on this track: he's double-tracked! 'Not bad!! Not bad at all': just genetically dirty!

'Best Batch Yet' (Van Vliet)

This has a heavy, slow riff with lead guitar. The voice is deep and deliberate.

We're 'the best batch yet'. 'You might think this is the finest pearl/But it's only cardboard balls seamed in glue'. I don't think this refers just to the band here, but more likely to all of mankind. 'We're the best batch yet' is meant sarcastically. We're all superficial and nowhere near as good as we think we are. The music meshes with clashing riffs, fabulous bass and the most incredible drumming. At times, the guitars deploy a call-and-answer approach. Don delivers his judgement like a shaman. 'White flesh waves to black', 'It is truly remarkable/We're the best batch yet': a bunch of phonies.

'Telephone' (Van Vliet)

This is delivered in a high-pitched burst of pure paranoia mimicking Antennae Jimmy Semens' delivery on 'The Blimp' or 'Pena' from *Trout Mask Replica*. It's Don's bad trip spent pulling a telephone apart looking for surveillance or control. He'd find plenty of it today. Paper and wire seem to symbolize civilization. Communication as personified by the telephone has robbed us of our freedoms. We can no longer live wild. Who knows what Don would make of this 21st-century age of social media, mobile phones, fake news and immersion in trivia. 'They' are out to get us was his key message. The guitar is spiky and barbed; the drums are like hard-edged concrete. The bass and other guitar are more mellow as a foil to counter aggression. The psychotic Beefheart releases his poetry in a great gush of breathless fear-ridden angst, apparently completely oblivious to the music.

'Flavor Bud Living' (Van Vliet)
This is another re-recording of a *Bat Chain Puller* song. Where John 'Drumbo' French delivered that rendition, here it's Gary Lucas' gentler version. John's was bright, clear and more angular. In their own way, both bring out this fabulous instrumental's melodic beauty.

'Sheriff Of Hong Kong' (Van Vliet)
Is this – as Bo Diddley sang about – 'Hong Kong, Mississippi'? Maybe, but this is a far more mystical and mythical place. It's not even Hong Kong China. The lyric refers to Gary Lucas' first wife Ling, who managed Don for a while. The spoken Chinese at the end translates as 'I love you, young lady'.

The introduction provides the entry point into a chaotic world of great complexity. The weighty drums congeal with the guitar and bass to set up a fabulous groove that evolves and changes but never loses fluidity. Over the top, Don's voice howls like a banshee – growling, shouting, whooping and pleading in strangled deranged rants before descending into incoherence. The Chinese gong punctuates everything. 'I don't know who I am, do you?'. Is it a stoned opium observation or a metaphysical question?

The backing is chaotic at first, but when you get lost in the mesmerizing jigsaw, you can allow your mind to follow the interweaving threads of all the components. Who or what is this Sheriff of Hong Kong? A shaman, a dealer or an acid trip? Perhaps a mystical guru. Whatever she is, she makes you fly.

'Making Love to A Vampire With A Monkey On My Knee' (Van Vliet)
Beefheart is sitting beside a pond in the moonlight, surrounded by nature, despairing at the world's dishonesty. He gives us a poem that speaks of futility, the frustration of life and the inherent impurity and corruption of our modern world. This is Beefheart in full flow, creating vivid images that convey subliminal messages through dense layers. It's like bringing the poetry of Rimbaud or Baudelaire into 21st-century culture with its addictions, distractions and putrid vacuousness. The poem is recited over music drenched with the same feeling of disquiet, anger and pointlessness.

A synthesized rhythm – like a windscreen wiper – sets a pattern for the sporadic drum and two guitars. The rhythm breaks up as the organ begins with ominous chords, followed by saxophone, a little marimba, becoming increasingly chaotic... and then gone. It's a chilling piece to end the album; quite disturbing.

Ice Cream for Crow (1982)

Personnel:

Don Van Vliet (Captain Beefheart): vocals, harmonica, soprano sax, Chinese gongs, prop horn

Jeff 'Moris' Tepper: steel appendage guitar, slide guitar, acoustic guitar

Richard 'Midnight Hatsize' Snyder: bass, marimba, viola

Gary 'Mantis' Lucas: glass finger guitar, slide guitar, guitar, national steel Duolian

Cliff R. Martinez: drums, shake bouquet, glass washboard, metal drums

Eric Drew Feldman: Rhodes piano, synthesizer bass

Studio: Warner Bros., North Hollywood, CA

Producer: Don Van Vliet

Production assistants: Jeff 'Moris' Tepper, Jan Van Vliet

Engineer: Phil Brown

Don Van Vliet: painting

Anton Corbijn: photography

Michael Hollyfield: art direction

Label: Virgin/Epic

The prevailing wisdom is that it's always best to go out on a high note, and that's precisely what the Captain did with this album. Once again there were important personnel changes. Drummer John 'Drumbo' French was out, replaced by Cliff R. Martinez. Gary Lucas was upgraded from a bit part to being integral to the band (as well as manager), and Richard 'Midnight Hatsize' Snyder took over on bass, and also played marimba and viola.

But there's a sad tale behind this album. The *Bat Chain Puller* tapes appeared to be suddenly available because Frank Zappa and Herb Cohen had resolved their legal issues. Don visited Frank to ask if he'd release the tapes so Don could release the unused tracks. Frank refused and treated Don in an offhand and condescending manner, which added to the ongoing rancour. A thwarted Beefheart then hurriedly had to set about writing new material and re-recording some of the early pieces.

From Bat Chain Puller, 'Human Totem Pole' (The 1000th And 10th Day Of The Human Totem Pole)' was re-recorded, and the a cappella poem '81 Poop Hatch' was used as it was. The old songs 'Semi-Multicolored Caucasian', 'The Past Sure Is Tense' and 'The Witch Doctor Life' were resurrected and recorded. This all led to a hodgepodge of material that could've been a recipe for disaster. Unexpectedly, it all came together in another complete triumph.

The cover features an original Don painting, with photographs of him and the band posing in the Mojave Desert. The band members look young and not at all weird. I'm not sure why he chose this particular painting for the cover. Given the album title, other paintings of his that feature the desert and crows might've been more appropriate. Perhaps he hadn't done any of those yet. The painting is an indication of where Don's head was. He was moving more into the art realm.

After this album, Don hardly recorded again, and only some stilted poems were ever released. There is speculation about why he left music behind. It's possible the symptoms of multiple sclerosis – from which he died in 2010 – were beginning to affect him, or perhaps his nerves, increasing agoraphobia and social anxiety (he found people and cities overwhelming) were to blame. On the other hand, perhaps he found art more rewarding and lucrative. Whatever the reasons (probably a combination), Don put aside his music career and returned to the art he'd been so good at in his childhood. Instead of sculpture, he became a successful exponent of abstract and expressionist art. His canvasses fetch high prices, and many of his admirers have no idea that this Don Van Vliet had ever been a rock musician known as Captain Beefheart.

'Ice Cream For Crow' (Van Vliet)
The album announces itself with a real driving number – a storming five minutes of high-octane funk. The bass, guitar and drums meld into a solid wall of pulsing sound with all the magnetism of 'Bat Chain Puller'. I love that squeaky harp on the outro!

The vocal starts in agonized, strangulated tones, warning us that it's going to get mighty hot during the day in this desert, but mighty cold at night. That crow's going to need sun cream in the day, and it'll get ice cream at night.

A great promo video was made of this number. Don and the band are miming, prancing and dancing in the desert to a backdrop of pylons, tumbleweeds and Joshua trees. They display a number of his fabulous paintings. MTV considered it too bizarre to broadcast, but New York's Museum of Modern Art celebrated the video, bought it for their collection, and have displayed it on many occasions.

'The Host The Ghost The Most Holy O' (Van Vliet)
Another hymn to the mess made of the planet: 'Why, not even a rustler'd have anything to do with this branded bum steer world'. It's one of Don's most brilliant poems – straightforward and nowhere near as opaque as many of his other masterpieces. The message is clear – we should listen to the sweet noise of nature instead of living in this dark oppression we've created for ourselves. 'Sing ye brothers and end this miserable thing'. Bring back the light.

The backing is fairly restrained. The slide guitar soars. Don recites the poem earnestly as the guitar plays a repeating descending phrase. I don't think Don has suddenly discovered religion: far from it. 'I can't darken your dark cross door no more'. I think this is a hymn to the host, and the host is the planet.

'Semi-Multicoloured' Caucasian (Van Vliet)
Don once said, 'We're all coloured, or you wouldn't be able to see anyone'. That says all you need to know about race.

This instrumental is quite atypical of Beefheart. Despite having quite a few weird noises and a modicum of strangeness, it sounds quite orthodox to my ears. It's jaunty, but nothing jagged or spiky. There are slow sections with strange-sounding guitar notes that build but don't seem to go anywhere. Towards the end, the music slows again, with another burst of peculiar guitar and some xylophone.

'Hey Garland, I Dig Your Tweed Coat' (Van Vliet)
The Captain's on form here with a slice of his best beat poetry – a collage of unrelated details that seem to describe a room using a microscope. The parts coalesce into a picture. There are some classic lines: 'And circles don't fly, they float'; 'From here to here it ain't far enough/But from here to here it's too short'. He's on the street surrounded by weird scenery, it's turning cold and he doesn't want to part with his tweed coat (bought from the goodwill store, smelling of mothballs). 'Who'd you look like underneath?'. The backing churns, guitars gel and the bass, bubbles, all merging into an unchanging amorphous sound over which Don recites his words.

'Evening Bell' (Van Vliet)
Another solo guitar instrumental, this time from Gary Lucas. It's a complex piece with all manner of technique and unusual tuning. Gary recorded another version at home that's more relaxed and has greater warmth. In the studio, Don wanted him to apply the 'exploding note theory': where 'Each note is separate from the others like bombs bursting in the air'.

'Cardboard Cutout Sundown' (Van Vliet)
Guitar and muffled drums lead to bursts of sound. Don sings about a desert scene, conjuring up one of those old film sets where they shot vintage cowboy movies. The guitar works away in the left channel while the band is doing something totally different in the right. They keep stopping and starting with faster rhythms.

Gary Lucas said the piece began as a Beefheart piano composition called 'Oat Hate'. Don whistled sections and based the drum sound on laden shopping bags swishing as they were swung around. Gary was told to play his piece with intense staccato rhythm using the exploding note theory without regard to the rest of the band. As they played live, Don – like a manic wizard – intuitively manipulated all the instruments and demanded (through their headphones) that the musicians stop and start to his command. Each musician played their individual composed section, oblivious to all others, as Don melded the piece into a coherent shape. Incredibly, towards the end, they found themselves linking up and playing the same motifs rhythmically and harmonically.

'The Past Sure Is Tense' (Van Vliet)
This rhythm is certainly not as jagged as most of Beefheart's work. But as soon as his voice comes into play – full of inflexions as ever – you know this is a

classic. He's howling, whooping and kicking up a dust cloud of noises. The number builds to a discordant finale with horns in the background and a burst of harmonica. The wordplay is at its best.

'Ink Mathematics' (Van Vliet)
A song of cerebral gymnastics with grey matter elastics, as Don plays with rhymes, making up new words if there's not a handy one to fit. The band sounds like the Magic Band of *Trout Mask Replica*, with clashing guitars and intricate drum patterns. The instruments are all in their own world, playing separate complex motifs but somehow melding.

'The Witch Doctor Life' (Van Vliet)
This was written around the time of *Shiny Beast (Bat Chain Puller)*, when the band recorded the song, but the results weren't good enough. Don sings his poem with real passion. The music is based around a beautiful melodic meshing of guitars with a strong and sympathetic rhythm section providing a heavy bottom end. Towards the end, the band plays briefly to a faster tempo and then slows, ultimately fading into silence; the result is magic.

The world is determined by magic. The lyric's shaman throws his bones and determines the future, making and breaking kings, while the mystical 'Mama Kangaroo' provides an 'insecure' refuge for the 'Beggars and drones and babies and bums and buzzards', from the forces that surround us. The bones sing of the eternity of silence.

'"81" Poop Hatch' (Van Vliet)
This was lifted directly from Bat Chain Puller and used here as an aural introduction to 'The Human Totem Pole', which has a similar spoken-word technique.

'The Thousandth and Tenth Day Of The Human Totem Pole' (Van Vliet)
This is a re-recording of the *Bat Chain Puller* song, but with a different feel. This is more sophisticated, gentle and relaxed. Don recites in a calmer manner. The band is very together as it enhances the poetry lines – although the horn rasps: adding a discord that's juxtaposed against the placid melodies. The voice is clear but sounds as if he's speaking within himself; very controlled. This version is less raw, with more of a jazz groove.

'Skeleton Makes Good' (Van Vliet)
Written in just one evening, this is possibly the album's best and most innovative track. Guitar starts the piece, but Don's voice cuts in with strangulated tones almost straight away as the band set up a complex lurching rhythm. The clearly accentuated guitar plays a delicate refrain throughout. At one point, most of the band stop, leaving just maracas and a melodic string of

guitar notes. Then they return with a steady rhythm and some odd cymbals. The number is slightly off-kilter, with a sinister feel.

The surreal lyrics talk of how there's so much to see in this world and the other universe of our dreams and nightmares. Don links the image of a skeleton, with nightmares: a motif that also appears in his paintings. Which is more real? Dreams or life?

The chiming picked guitar finishes; a cowbell rattles and fades to nothing. The Captain has written his last notes; sung his last words. It's over.

EP release

'Ice Cream For Crow'/'Tropical Hot Dog Night'/'Run Paint Run Run'/'Light Reflected Off The Oceands Of The Moon'
Virgin released this EP in 1982. The first three tracks were taken from the albums *Ice Cream For Crow, Shiny Beast (Bat Chain Puller)* and *Doc At The Radar Station*. 'Light Reflected Off The Oceands Of The Moon' was an unreleased track from the *Ice Cream for Crow* sessions.

'Light Reflected Off The Oceands Of The Moon' (Van Vliet)

Don's unrestricted sax is plastered over this instrumental version of 'Hey Garland, I Dig Your Tweed Coat', smothering it with raucous noise. This fine piece of abstract aural sculpture was not included on *Ice Cream For Crow*. It's four minutes of instrumental avant-garde free-form jazz as only Beefheart can do, composed around two guitars holding their own riffs against a complex drum rhythm. The bass provides both a bottom end and solid spine behind Don's honking, wailing horns. It's a discordant, chaotic splurge. It's wonderful, even if it isn't easy on the ear.

Don finished his music career with one of his best albums. He left rock music behind and developed a lucrative career as a surrealist/impressionist artist.

That was it. Except, it wasn't quite. Over subsequent years, a whole industry has grown around albums of outtakes, obscure rarities and live performances. A multitude of bands still cover the Captain's material. Many individual Magic Band members have produced their own albums, clearly displaying Beefheart's influence. The Magic Band reformed in 2003 to perform live shows and produce albums of Captain Beefheart material. Those of us who saw their concerts or bought the albums, know they were not by any stretch of the imagination a tribute band; they were the real thing, just, sadly, missing the Captain.

The Compilations

A Carrot Is as Close As A Rabbit Gets To A Diamond (1993)
Label: Virgin

A compilation taken from the Virgin albums *Unconditionally Guaranteed*, *Bluejeans & Moonbeams*, *Shiny Beast (Bat Chain Puller)*, *Doc at the Radar Station* and Ice Cream For Crow. The tracks seem to have been randomly thrown together, along with weird snippets of dialogue that have nothing to do with the songs. Most peculiar. The one track that makes it special is 'Light Reflected On The Oceands Of The Moon': previously only available on the 1982 'Ice Cream For Crow' EP, and only now making its CD debut.

Tracklist: 'Sugar Bowl', 'The Past Sure Is Tense', 'Happy Love Song', 'The Floppy Boot Stomp', 'Blue Jeans And Moonbeams', 'Run Paint Run Run', 'This Is The Day', 'Tropical Hot Dog Night', 'Observatory Crest', 'The Host, The Ghost, The Most Holy-O', 'Harry Irene', 'I Got Love On My Mind', 'Pompadour Swamp', 'Love Lies', 'Sheriff Of Hong Kong', 'Further Than We've Gone', 'Candle Mambo', 'Light Reflected Off The Oceands Of The Moon', 'A Carrot Is As Close As A Rabbit Gets To A Diamond'

The Dust Blows Forwards And The Dust Blows Back (1999)
Label: Rhino

An interesting double CD spanning from 1966 to 1982, with tracks from each album except for *Mirror Man*. There are some rarities, such as the first single 'Diddy Wah Diddy', 'Hard Workin' Man' from the film Blue Collar, and 'Light Reflecting On The Oceands Of The Moon'. This has been assembled with care and thought, is a good place to start for an overview of Don's work, and comes with a well-written booklet.

Tracklist. Disc 1: 'Diddy Wah Diddy', 'Frying Pan', 'Electricity', 'Abba Zaba', 'Beatle Bones 'N' Smokin' Stones', 'Safe As Milk', 'Moonlight On Vermont', 'Ella Guru', 'Old Fart At Play', 'Sugar 'N' Spikes', 'Orange Claw Hammer', 'My Human Gets Me Blues', 'China Pig', *Lick My Decals Off Baby*', 'Woe Is Uh Me Bop', 'I Wanna Find Me A Woman That'll Hold My Big Toe Till I Have To Go', 'The Smithsonian Institute Blues', 'I'm Gonna Booglarize You Baby', 'Click Clack', 'Grow Fins', 'When It Blows Its Stacks', 'Little Scratch', 'Big Eyed Beans From Venus', 'Golden Birdies'

Disc 2: 'Nowadays A Woman's Gotta Hit A Man', 'Low Yo Yo Stuff', 'Too Much Time', 'My Head Is My Only House Unless It Rains', *Clear Spot*', 'Upon The My Oh My', 'Party Of Special Things To Do', 'Sam With The Showing Scalp Flat Top', 'Debra Kadabra', 'Hard Workin' Man', 'Bat Chain Puller', 'The Floppy Boot Stomp', 'Tropical Hot Dog Night', 'Owed T'Alex', 'Hot Head', 'Ashtray Heart', 'Sue Egypt', 'Making Love To A Vampire With A Monkey On My Knee', 'Ice Cream For Crow', 'The Past Sure Is Tense', 'Light Reflected Off The Oceands Of The Moon'

The Best Of Captain Beefheart & the Magic Band/The Best Of The Virgin & Liberty Years (2002)
Labels: Virgin/Liberty
This strange tracklist was selected from the Liberty and Virgin albums *Strictly Personal*, *Unconditionally Guaranteed*, *Bluejeans & Moonbeams*, *Shiny Beast (Bat Chain Puller)*, *Doc at the Radar Station* and Ice Cream For Crow.

Tracklist: 'Safe As Milk', 'Gimme Dat Harp Boy', 'Kandy Korn', 'Upon The My-O-My', 'New Electric Ride', 'Party Of Special Things To Do', 'Twist Ah Luck', 'Blue Jeans And Moonbeams', 'The Floppy Boot Stomp', 'Bat Chain Puller', 'Run Paint Run Run', 'Hot Head', 'Ashtray Heart', *'Ice Cream for Crow* ', 'The Past Sure Is Tense'

Hothead – Introducing... Captain Beefheart (2003)
Labels: Virgin/Liberty

Yet another compilation from the Liberty and Virgin albums *Strictly Personal*, *Unconditionally Guaranteed*, *Bluejeans & Moonbeams*, *Shiny Beast (Bat Chain Puller)*, *Doc at the Radar Station* and *Ice Cream For Crow*. Half of these tracks were on the compilation released the previous year!

Tracklist: 'Safe As Milk', 'Upon The My-O-My', 'Son Of *Mirror Man* – Mere Man', 'Party Of Special Things To Do', 'The Floppy Boot Stomp', 'Tropical Hot Dog Night', 'Hot Head', 'This Is The Day', 'You Know You're A Man', 'Ice Cream For Crow', 'Pompadour Swamp', 'Suction Prints', 'Semi-Multicolored Caucasian', 'Gimme Dat Harp Boy', 'Making Love To A Vampire With A Monkey on My Knee', 'Sheriff Of Hong Kong', 'The Witch Doctor Life'

Electricity (2015)
Label: Yellow
Tracks from the Buddah Years, selected from *Safe As Milk*, *Strictly Personal* and *Mirror Man*, including outtakes from the early years. It was also released as a 16-song single album minus the last three tracks.

Tracklist. Disc 1: 'Sure 'Nuff 'N Yes, I Do', ', 'Zig Zag Wanderer', 'Dropout Boogie', 'I'm Glad', 'Electricity', 'Yellow Brick Road', 'Abba Zaba', 'Plastic Factory', 'Trust Us ', 'Beatle Bones 'N' Smokin' Stone', 'Moody Liz', 'Big Black Baby Shoes', 'Gimme Dat Harp Boy', 'Dirty Blue Gene

Disc 2: 'Tarotplane', 'Kandy Korn', 'Safe As Milk (Take 5)', '25th Century Quaker', 'Korn Ring Finger'

Official/Unofficial Rarities, Outtakes and Semi-bootlegs

If You Got Ears (1994)
An unofficial release of rarities and outtakes spanning most of Don's career. The standout track is the great obscene version of 'Hard Workin' Man'.

Tracklist: 'Hard Workin' Man' (Blue Collar 7" version), 'Moody Liz' (*Strictly Personal* outtake), 'Odd Jobs' (*Bat Chain Puller* outtake)', '*Mirror Man*' (Drury Lane, 1974)', 'Torture' (Bongo Fury outtake)', 'Little Scratch' (Outtake)', 'Funeral Hill' (Outtake)', 'Dirty Blue Gene' (Early version)', 'Picture Of Mahavishnu' (Live)', 'Light Reflected Off The Oceands Of The Moon' (Rare 12")', 'Evil' (Avalon Ballroom, 1966)', 'Flash Gordon's Ape' (Alternate vocal No. 1)', 'Lick My Decals Off, Baby' (Instrumental)', 'Hard Workin' Man' (Obscene version)

The Early Years 1959-1969 (1995)
First released as a limited edition of 500 copies, then later re-released without limit and with a different cover. Both were produced in Luxembourg to evade copyright infringement. The copyright laws in some countries allow this purloining of material. There are tracks from Don's early years with Frank Zappa, live recordings from 1966 (Avalon Ballroom), alternative takes from *Safe As Milk*, *It Comes To You In A Brown Paper Bag*, and recordings from the *Trout Mask Replica* house rehearsals. A number of these tracks came out in higher quality on the officially-released Grow Fins box set of rarities. All of the Avalon Ballroom material was later released on the CD Live 1966-1967.

Of particular interest are the historic early pieces with Frank Zappa. They sound exactly like what they are: two High School kids playing around with musical ideas. But their potential is obvious. They were hugely ambitious. As early as 1963, they were composing a teenage rock opera, producing film scripts and creating adventurous sci-fi projects, all with the hope of securing a record deal and becoming successful.

'Lost In A Whirlpool' (Zappa, Van Vliet)
This is the earliest recording of Don, made on a tape machine in a classroom at Antelope Valley High School in 1959, with Frank and Bobby Zappa on guitars. Don was only a teenager, but his voice already had an extraordinary blues vibe. The juvenile content (about being flushed down a toilet and chased by a large brown turd) is weird: a forewarning of what was to come. This track was also released on the Frank Zappa album *The Lost Episodes*.

'I Was A Teenage Maltshop' (Zappa, Van Vliet)
In 1963, Frank and Don set about recording a teenage opera. They offered it to Dot Records, but without success. The recording was made in Frank's

Studio Z in Cucamonga. This is a short episode from that opera, featuring Don announcing, 'I was a teenage maltshop' and laughing before the piano-based music kicks in.

The extract also appears on Frank's *The Lost Episodes* and *Mystery Disc* albums.

'Metal Man Has Won His Wings' (Zappa, Van Vliet)

Recorded at Studio Z in 1963/1964. Don presents himself as Captain Beefheart for the very first time: 'Hello kids, it's your old friend Captain Beefheart. You know me. the magic man'. He announces the teenage opera in a phoney showman voice, reading words straight from a comic book (issue 7 of the DC title *Metal Men*) that was pinned to the wall of the corridor where he was singing. Don and Frank's band The Soots, slide into an excellent Booker T. & the M.G.'s-type groove with Don interjecting sounds and repeating words.

'Tupelo Mississippi' (John Lee Hooker), 'Somebody's Walking' (Howlin' Wolf), 'Old Folks Boogie' (Van Vliet), 'Evil' (Howlin' Wolf), Blues Jam (Van Vliet)

These tracks are from the radio broadcast of the 1966 Avalon Ballroom concert. This is before the band recorded their first album, when they were still predominantly a blues outfit. Most of their material at this time was made up of blues covers of Howlin' Wolf and John Lee Hooker, but you can hear Don already putting his own brand on the music.

A number of these tracks appear on *Grow Fins* with improved quality, and the whole concert was later released on *Captain Beefheart & His Magic Band Live 1966-1967*.

'Out Of The Frying Pan' (Alt version) (Van Vliet)

An alternative take from the A&M session. It's not very different from the version that came out as the B-side of the second single 'Moonchild'. It has a bright, exciting sound with brilliant harmonica-playing.

'Almost Grown' (Chuck Berry)

A previously unreleased cover. It's interesting but has poor sound quality, though it has some great harmonica-playing.

'Call On Me' (Slow version)

A slow moody, soulful performance of a classic song. It's a shame the production isn't clearer. A better quality version is available on Grow Fins.

'Sure Nuff 'N' Yes I Do' (John Peel Sessions 1968)

John Peel was their biggest fan, and this great version comes from a live Peel Session recorded during the band's first UK tour.

'Moody Liz' (Rare acetate version)

This acetate was made because it was the song was considered for a single. But it was later rejected and not even included on the Strictly Personal album. The song is an extended, with guitar parts that are quite different to other recordings. There is a little 'Safe As Milk' riff in the middle of the jam.

'Korn Ring Finger' (Van Vliet)

Possibly an outtake from the *Mirror Man* sessions, but the notes say it's from *Safe As Milk*. A better quality version was added as a bonus track on the *Safe As Milk* CD reissue, and also appears on *Grow Fins*.

'Frownland', 'Ella Guru', 'Hair Pie – Bake 1'/'Hair Pie – Bake 2', 'Pachuco Cadaver', 'Sugar 'N' Spikes'

These 'bush' recordings are from an instrumental run-through of the album prior to the studio recordings. You can hear how tight the band was, and without the vocals, the instrumentation is clear. The arrangements are more obvious and the complexity of the pieces are laid bare. These all appear on Grow Fins.

'Neon Meat Dream Of A Octofish'

Don's recites above a chaotic, discordant jumble of loud instruments that sound like they're fighting with each other. The drums and bass hold it together. This is more frenzied than the official version. This version has ever been released anywhere else.

'The Blimp' (Edit), 'Candy Man', 'China Pig'

A short extract of Antennae Jimmy Semens singing 'The Blimp', with Magic Band backing. This is how it might've sounded had Frank not used the pre-existing Mothers Of Invention backing track on the album. This segues into Don messing about with Doug Moon.

'Well Well Well'

The only version I've heard with Rockette Morton singing, which gives the song a totally different vibe, peculiarly reminding me of Woody Guthrie, but with a strange jazzy backing.

Stand Up To Be Discontinued (1992)

This started as a book/catalogue produced for the 1992 travelling art exhibition, which included the original release of the six poems later incorporated in the Pearls Before Swine book.

This is the book for Don's artwork – originally published in three large editions: paperback, hardback and hardback with signed print. It contains 63 artworks, facsimiles of several music paper interviews, and six essays on Don's art: one by Pearls Before Swine author Luca Ferrari.

Pearls Before Swine (1996)

Sonic books

A little CD-size book of 118 pages – half Italian and half English. It's a series of essays on various Beefheartian subjects – mainly art and poetry – with photos, sketches and paintings.

Accompanying the book is a miniature CD on which Don recites six poems. His delivery came as quite a shock to those of us who were familiar with him. But that made them all the more poignant. The Captain sounded frail, his voice faltering as he was obviously struggling. This filled me with great sadness, but I can now listen and appreciate the determination that went into reciting the poems.

That 'fallin' ditch' was not going to rob him of his intrinsic being. He was resolute.

'Fallin' Ditch' (Circa 1969)

This is a lyric from *Trout Mask Replica*. Like all these poems, Don reads with great pathos and emotion, accentuated by laboured effort. The 'fallin' ditch' is a metaphor for either death or depression, or perhaps both. Despite his now-obvious physical handicap, he was never going to allow himself to fall into that ditch. The effects of the multiple sclerosis were clearly showing, but his defiance shone through.

'The Tired Plain'

This was written before 1970. We move from pathos to humour with this description of a bra, and a cowboy's hand reaching for a grope.

'Skeleton Makes Good' (1982)

An observation of life, dreams, reality and love, taken from *Ice Cream For Crow*. This time it's read as a poem. This skeleton has a crush on you, both physically and emotionally.

'Safe Sex Drill' (Circa 1990)

We're back to the humour – a toilet paper roll: a tube with a hole. Male or female?

'Tulip' (28 September 1991)

What is he looking at and describing? It could be...? It could be...? No idea.

'Gil' (Prior to 1969)

This starts with Bub and Gil. Bub goes off with Mat. Fun and trouble. Bub comes back to Gil. Bub, Mat and Gil have fun. Sex and the sweet scent of love. This could be about the Zappas – the Hot Rats album is dedicated to (Frank and Gail's son) Dweezil, Gil and Bub. Gail Zappa is probably Gil, and Bub is possibly Moon Unit.

The Lost Episodes – Frank Zappa (1996)
Label: Rykodisc
Frank Zappa was working on this compilation before he died. It consists largely of unreleased material stretching back to 1958, featuring five tracks recorded with Don.

'Lost In A Whirlpool' (Zappa, Van Vliet)
As on the The Early Years 1959-1969.

'Tiger Roach' (Zappa, Van Vliet)
Recorded circa 1961/1962, and is as weird as it gets. 'This album is not available to the public. Even if it was, you wouldn't want to listen to it', Don says as the track featuring a great R&B rhythm hurtles along at a rate of knots, with Don clearing his throat, gurgling, and having fun making a series of loud noises as weirdly as he can, then pouring forth a string of word associations. The voice is less mature, but many Beefheartisms are already there.

'I'm A Band Leader' (Zappa, Van Vliet)
We're now in 1969. Don recites this humorous piece. It's more a comedy sketch than a poem.

'Alley Cat' (Zappa, Van Vliet)
This is more like the Beefheart we know, at least vocal-wise, although the song structure is more Zappa than Beefheart. It's a standard R&B format, with some strangeness thrown in. Zappa's on guitar, and the rest of the band is Beefheart's.

'The Grand Wazoo' (Zappa, Van Vliet)
Another track from 1969. Beefheart recites a poem about being the Grand Wazoo, over Zappa-ish weirdness that would fit very nicely on any of Frank's 1960s albums. There are plentiful effects. The voice is vari-sped as the band cut loose with the weirdest noises they can come up with.

Cheap Thrills – Frank Zappa (1998)
Label: Rykodisc
This is a budget compilation of various Zappa tracks, with 'The Torture Never Stops' featuring Captain Beefheart on vocals and harmonica. This is included on Zappa's *You Can't Do That On Stage Anymore Vol. 4*.

'The Torture Never Stops' (Frank Zappa)
A scary track that lasts nearly ten minutes and is based around a repeating riff over words about the stinking dungeon of the Evil Prince, where the flies are green and buzzin, the stench makes even the stones choke, and the torture never stops. The track features Denny Walley and Frank Zappa on guitar. Don

sings with authority and plays harmonica. A fabulous rendition. A music video was made of the song, graphically showing how a regime can control and even torture us.

Mystery Disc – Frank Zappa (1998)

The album contains a few early Beefheart oddities which have appeared before. There is 'Opening Night Party At Studio Z' (a collage of music and talk from the event that Beefheart attended), 'I Was A Teenage Maltshop' and 'Metal Man Has Won His Wings', which is split into two with the introduction called 'The Birth Of Captain Beefheart'.

Grow Fins – Rarities 1965-1982 (5 CD box set) (1999)
Label: Revenant

In my view, this is as much a historic document as a music album because of the way the information and music was collated and is presented. The box set is in the form of a small hardback book within a lavish, glossy slipcase covered with purple flowers and inset with photos of the band from the *Trout Mask Replica* photo shoot. The book contains 112 pages of notes and information, along with cardboard cases for the five discs. The contents are a treasure trove of joy for hardened Beefheart fans. There's everything we could desire – 4 hours of music, being 78 outtakes, live performance, demos and banter: Beefheart heaven. There's also a series of demos from the period circa the first album, live radio sessions, the *Trout Mask Replica* rehearsals, an enhanced CD of videos, and an assortment of odds and sods.

Disc one: Just Got Back From the City (1965-1967)

A great CD packed with interesting material dating from before the first album. That was when the band was a psyched-up R&B band who could blow any other R&B band off the planet. Their jagged sound (based on Howlin' Wolf's deep, resonant voice) ideally suited Don's subterranean singing. Other ingredients – such as psychedelia, poetic wordplay and quirky avant-garde – were beginning to infiltrate the music.

The tracks navigate the path to that first album. You can hear the building blocks slotting into place. There are cuts that didn't make it to the album ('Obeah Man', 'Just Got Back From The City'), live blues tracks from the Avalon Ballroom in 1966 ('Tupelo', 'Evil') and demos ('Sure 'Nuff 'N' Yes I Do', 'Yellow Brick Road'). Together they provide insight into how the band evolved. This is the primaeval coalescence of blues, soul and acid that gave rise to the Captain's incredible discography and spawned the most exciting live band I've ever seen.

Tracklist. Disc one: 'Obeah Man' (1966 demo), 'Just Got Back From The City' (1966 demo), 'I'm Glad' (1966 demo), 'Triple Combination' (1966 demo), 'Here I Am I Always Am' (Early 1966 demo), 'Here I Am I Always Am' (Later 1966 demo), 'Somebody in My Home' (Live Avalon Ballroom 1966), 'Tupelo'

(Live Avalon Ballroom 1966), 'Evil' (Live Avalon Ballroom 1966), 'Old Folks Boogie' (Live Avalon Ballroom 1967), 'Call On Me' (1965 demo), 'Sure 'Nuff 'N' Yes I Do' (1967 demo), 'Yellow Brick Road' (1967 demo)

Disc Two: Electricity (1968)

This picks up where the first CD stops and contains scintillating live performances of songs from the first album, with a couple of forays into material destined for It Comes To You Wrapped In A Brown Paper Bag. The heavy blues base is still there in extended versions of 'You're Going To Need Somebody On Your Bond' and 'Rollin' 'N' Tumblin'', but it ventures into psychedelia with 'Electricity' and 'Sure Nuff 'N' Yes I Do'.

The live tracks were mainly recorded in Europe on that first tour, and their strength and power is awesome. John French provides a powerhouse of rhythm which was to become an essential element, while Alex Snouffer and Jeff Cotton create snarling blues slide riffs with metal finger picks: fierce and distinctive.

The 11-minute live version of 'Rollin' 'N' Tumblin' recorded at Frank Freeman's dance studio in Kidderminster shows clearly how they took the basic blues riffs and adapted them.

Tracklist: Disc two: 'Electricity' (Live at Cannes 1968), 'Sure Nuff 'N' Yes I Do' (Live at Cannes 1968), 'Rollin 'N' Tumblin'' (Kidderminster 1968), 'Electricity' (Kidderminster 1968), 'You're Gonna Need Somebody on Your Bond' (Kidderminster 1968), 'Kandy Korn' (Kidderminster 1968), 'Korn Ring Finger' (1967 demo)

Disc three: Trout Mask House Sessions (1969)

With nothing from the *Mirror Man* or *Strictly Personal* era, we jump ahead to *Trout Mask Replica*. We've exploded straight from the edgy psychedelic blues into another dimension; another universe altogether. This one is strewn with weirdness – free-form jazz, discordant noise, interweaving polyrhythms, slashing guitar riffs playing off each other, and complex drum rhythms. The jump is enormous. We're now getting a glimpse of a surreal, acid-drenched world. We're in the house. The band had been rehearsing non-stop for up to 18 hours a day. They ate and slept music. Well, in truth, they didn't do much eating or sleeping; the atmosphere was oppressive. Don had turned from hard taskmaster into tyrant. He was driving this new avant-garde style to perfection. Nothing like this had ever been heard. This was the most out-there sound ever created.

The group were tighter than any of the Captain's bands had ever been. The recordings are rudimentary. These were rehearsals for the forthcoming studio recordings. The band were honing their instrumental parts. Don was not singing or laying down his horn parts: they would be added later in the studio. What we have here are the instrumental versions of virtually the whole *Trout*

Mask Replica album. Without the vocals and horn, the arrangements, precision and complexity are exposed in a fascinating insight.

Tracklist: Disc three: 'Hobo Chang Ba And Dachau Blues Tuning Up', 'Bush Recording', 'Hair Pie: Bake 1', 'Hair Pie: Bake 2', 'Noodling', 'Hobo Chang Ba', 'Hobo practice', 'Hobo Chang Ba (Take 2)', 'Dachau Blues', 'Old Fart At Play', 'Noodling', 'Pachuco Cadaver', 'Sugar 'N' Spikes', 'Noodling', 'Sweet Sweet Bulbs', 'Frownland' (Take 1)', 'Frownland', 'Noodling', 'Ella Guru', 'Silence', 'She's Too Much For My Mirror', 'Noodling', 'Steal Softly Thru Snow', 'Noodling', 'My Human Gets Me Blues', 'Noodling', 'When Big Joan Sets Up', 'Silence', 'Candy Man', 'China Pig'

Disc four: Trout Mask House Sessions Pt. 2 (Enhanced CD)

Disc four is an enhanced CD of some audio pieces, with a collection of video performances from key moments. As film of the band in action is scarce, these are extremely precious. The disc gives more insight into life at the *Trout Mask Replica* house with a few fly-on-the-wall conversations – interesting to listen to once or twice. The guts of the CD are those video gems spanning from 1968 to 1973 – two superb early songs from Cannes (if only we had a full performance!), two from Lick My Decals Off, Baby and one from *The Spotlight Kid*: far too few, but we're lucky to have them.

Tracklist: Disc four: 'Blimp Playback', 'Herb Alpert', 'Septic Tank', 'We'll Overdub It 3 Times'

Disc four video material:

'Electricity', ' Sure Nuff 'N Yes I Do' (Live Cannes Beach 1968), 'Click Clack' (Live Bataclan, Paris 1973), 'When Big Joan Sets Up', 'Woe Is Uh Me Bop', 'Bellerin Plain' (Detroit Tubeworks program, winter 1970/1971), 'She's Too Much For My Mirror', 'My Human Gets Me Blues' (Live Amougies 1969)

Disc five: Captain Beefheart & His Magic Band Grow Fins (1969-1981)

Disc five is a mixed bag of flotsam and jetsam accumulated over the years. The sound quality varies and the organisation is haphazard, but it's full of interesting pieces – like the a cappella blasting blues extract from 'Black Snake Moan' and various blues-harp snippets that Don did for live radio. There's weird performance poetry ('Spitball Scalped Uh Baby'), plus various demos and live performances. The strangest are probably the mellotron improvisations.

Among some inferior pieces, are a number of gems – an extraordinary radio performance of 'Orange Claw Hammer' featuring Frank Zappa on acoustic guitar (which makes it sound like a sea shanty), and a piano demo of 'Odd Jobs', which is extraordinarily beautiful. This CD is the most difficult to listen to, but it is well worth the effort.

Tracklist: Disc five: 'My Human Gets Me Blues' (Live Amougies 1969), 'When Big Joan Sets Up' (Live Detroit Tubeworks 1971), 'Woe Is Uh Me Bop' (Live Detroit Tubeworks 1971), 'Bellerin Plain (Live Detroit Tubeworks 1971), 'Black Snake Moan I'(KHSU 1972), 'Grow Fins' (Live Bickershaw 1972), 'Black Snake Moan II' (WBCN 1972), 'Spitball Scalped Uh Baby' (Live Bickershaw 1972), 'Harp Boogie I' (WBCN 1972), 'One Red Rose That I Mean' (Town Hall, New York 1972), 'Harp Boogie II' (WBCN 1972), 'Natchez Burning' (WBCN 1972), 'Harp Boogie III' (Radio phone-in 1972), 'Click Clack' (Paris 1973), 'Orange Claw Hammer' (Radio with Zappa on acoustic guitar 1975), 'Odd Jobs' (Don piano demo 1976), 'Odd Jobs' (Band demo 1976), 'Vampire Suite' (Work tapes/ live 1980), 'Mellotron Improv' (Live 1978), 'Evening Bell' (Don piano demo 1981), 'Evening Bell' (Lucas work tape 1981), 'Mellotron Improv' (Live 1980), 'Flavor Bud Living (Live 1981)

An unofficial CD titled *Trout Mask House Sessions 1969* was released in 2017 on the Grey Scale label. It had 29 tracks from the house, including most of what was on Grow Fins.

Riding Some Kind Of Unusual Skull Sleigh (2004)
Label:Rhino Handmade
This came out as a ridiculously lavish box set costing over £500! It consisted of a signed etching, two books, a CD of recited poems and words, and a DVD of a short film called *Some Yo-Yo Stuff*. It was not great value for money. The CD contains 34 minutes of poems/spoken-word snippets recorded between 1977 and 1999 on Don's tape recorder – and, as you might expect, they have ambient noise and varying levels of quality. I can see why this is called *Riding Some Kind Of Unusual Skull Sleigh*, because it feels like a trip through Don's mind, rushing down the slippery slopes of his brain inside his skull.

'Guitars, Wood Guitars' (Dec 1977) (Van Vliet)
Hilarious wordplay as Don tries to express his musical ideas – 'Vanilla pudding shaking', 'Little more shoe polish' – with some singing and noises. Somehow John French and Bill Harkleroad were meant to create musical arrangements out of these phrases. Amazingly, they did!

'Away From Survival' (Dec 1977) (Van Vliet)
There are various clicks as the recorder is turned on and off, and we hear fragments of asides as they travel in the car – some whistling, singing, talking and other sounds. It's an insight into how a musical composition might come together.

'The I Saw Shop' (Dec 1977) (Van Vliet)
'Sue, I'm behind you', says Don to his mother. He's playing with words as he puts together a poem about window art in Lancaster.

'Flat Mattress' (Dec 1977) (Van Vliet)

This piece gives a little more insight into how compositions might come together. Don is singing, playing with his voice, humming, deeply growling and spouting absurd words. In an unusually strange voice, he recites, 'Pulling the jello tooth out of an ice and glass skull'.

'Parachoke Stare' (Jan 17, 1978) (Van Vliet)

Here, Don whistles and sings. The poem is sung in order to record it: not as a concert performance.

'The Sand Failure' (1980) (Van Vliet)

Sax plays in the background as Don recites a poem and whistles.

'Geometry Street' (May 17, 1982) (Van Vliet)

There's sax playing in a bar. Someone's puked. Don's whistling a tune and practicing some words: 'Frank mathematics'.

'The Word Crawled Over The Razor Blade' (June 1 1982) (Van Vliet)

This sounds like a lively gathering of friends, with someone playing guitar. Don recites words similar to *Trout Mask Replica* poetry.

'Sit Through This' (Jun 1, 1982) (Van Vliet)

Don is singing fun words in a room with birds chirping in the background.

'Seaweed Beard Foam Bone Tree' (Dec 7, 1983) (Van Vliet)

A recited nautical poem with a tapping rhythm and whistles.

'The Thin Wood Door' (Aug 1999) (Van Vliet)

Not so much a thin wood door, as a slither of laboured words.

The Spotlight Kid Outtakes (2020)

Label: Sutra, Recorded at the Record Plant, 1971

Another semi-official release. Some of the various sessions from Amigo Studios in L.A. were leaked, and a serious Beefheart collector bought them. There was a wealth of material: full songs, instrumentals and alternate versions. Some of these songs ended up being recorded for future albums. Others were never used. A bootleg album was circulated. As more material was accessed, this single bootleg became a double, then a triple, and finally a four-CD set. Sutra Records released the first CD of outtakes. The other three CDs have yet to be officially released.

It's clear from these outtakes that Don's voice is right at its peak. These are effortless and they flow. The arrangements are more orthodox than we are used to, and the performances are relaxed. It seems like Don and the band are feeling their way into the new songs and trying out things as they go along. This gives a different type of listening experience. If these tracks were going to be included on the album, I think a lot more work would have to have gone into them. As it is they still work brilliantly just the way they are and the sound quality is perfect. It strikes me how dissimilar these early versions were to those later developed for *Clear Spot*, *Doc at the Radar Station* and Ice Cream For Crow. The words and song structures make for different entities.

'Drink Paint Run Run' (Van Vliet)

A change of words and a totally different feel to the song that ended up on Doc At The Radar Station. The band gets into a really great groove with that bass bouncing along. With so few words, it does get a tad repetitive, which gives it the feel of a demo. Nonetheless, the track is a fabulous seven-minute jam worthy of any album.

'Seam Crooked Sam' (Version 2) (Van Vliet)

Don tells this story perfectly, to a backing of blues harp, maracas and what sounds like hand-drumming on a guitar case. Terrific.

'Dirty Blue Gene' (Version 1) (Van Vliet)

This comes out as a totally different song. I love that dirty guitar riff, the interaction with the second guitar, and the harmonica at the end.

'Sun Zoom Spark' (Version 3) (Van Vliet)

While this has some spiky guitar, and Drumbo's drumming sets up a great rockin' rhythm, Don's delivery is so restrained that the effect is more relaxed than the version on *Clear Spot*.

'Kiss Me My Love' (Van Vliet)

A love song sung to a simple guitar backing with some marimba and drums back in the mix.

'Funeral Hill' (Version 1) (Van Vliet)

We're back into a heavy swampy blues, with Don's vocal delivered in the deepest register. There are ominous drums, sustained guitar notes and wailing harmonica. The track throbs with intensity as Don growls his chilling vocal straight out of a Hammer House of Horror movie. It's a song about death 'laying flowers on you on Funeral Hill': a precursor to 'There ain't no Santa Claus on the Evening Stage' from *The Spotlight Kid*.

'Harry Irene' (Jazz guitar version) (Van Vliet)

A sleazy, late-night adaptation with brushed drums, two quiet jazz guitars and Don singing tenderly in a soulful voice before tailing off with some whistling. This arrangement suits the song.

'Open Pins' (Improved sound) (Van Vliet)
An interesting instrument combination, with the bass leading the piece with fluid strings. Percussion, (wood block and marimba) gels with a simple repeating guitar refrain, creating a mesmeric rhythm and cyclic flow. Highly original.

'Dual & Abdul' (Van Vliet)
An instrumental experimental jam with an Eastern flavour, varying rhythms, wah-wah, and stops and starts.

'Semi-Multicoloured Caucasian' (Version 2) (Van Vliet)
A light and delicate marimba-led instrumental with an orthodox structure and a melodic sound.

'Balladino' (Van Vliet)
Another light instrumental with guitar and keyboard.

'Clear Spot' (Instrumental) (Van Vliet)
A slow, heavy guitar riff and drum rhythm with marimba sprinkled over it. It's nothing like the *Clear Spot* version.

'Circumstances' (Van Vliet)
This is much slower, less frenetic, far more bluesy, pared-back and atmospheric than the *Clear Spot* version. The intense, anguished vocal is sung over bass and drums. The harmonica and marimba create a totally different feel.

'I'm Gonna Booglarize You, Baby' (Instrumental) (Van Vliet)
A similar arrangement to that on *Clear Spot*, but less heavy. This takes away from the swampy feel, but emphasises the fabulous guitar riffs and highlights the solos.

'Low Yo Yo Stuff' (Instrumental) (Van Vliet)
This is a slow version, hardly recognisable from the *Clear Spot* song. The arrangement is centred on the guitar and marimba interaction, with intricate drum patterns and plenty of bass. There is a little dirty riff, but it tails off into a repeating refrain that gets a tad monotonous.

'Semi-Multicoloured Caucasian' (Version 1) (Van Vliet)
Another track based around the guitar and marimba combo that Don seems to like for its clash of tones. It's an instrumental that sounds pleasant enough but is uninspiring.

'Little Scratch' (Version 2) (Van Vliet)
The album finishes with a track full of pizzazz that sounds rather 1950s-ish to me. It's an R&B sound complete with blues harp and a rousing chorus from the band; a great little number.

The 4-CD version consists of these plus more of the same – all good-quality unreleased tracks, alternative and early versions, instrumentals and blues jams. It's unclear why the original album wasn't released as at least a double: there was more than enough excellent material.

Sun Zoom Spark (2014)

Personnel:
Don Van Vliet 'Captain Beefheart': vocals, harmonica
John French 'Drumbo': drums, percussion
Bill Harkleroad 'Zoot Horn Rollo': guitar, slide guitar
Mark Boston 'Rockette Morton': bass
Art Tripp 'Ed Marimba/Ted Cactus': drums, percussion, marimba, piano, harpsichord
Elliot Ingber 'Winged Eel Fingerling': guitar
Recorded at the Record Plant, Los Angeles
Producers: Don Van Vliet, Phil Schier
Label: Rhino/Reprise

There was much excitement in Beefheartland in the weeks leading up to this release. Not only was there anticipation over the three excellent remasters of *Lick My Decals Off, Baby*, *The Spotlight Kid* and *Clear Spot*, but there was speculation about what would be on the box set's fourth disc: Outtakes from 1970-1972. We were about to be wowed by more Spotlight Kid outtakes! Amazingly they were quite different from those already out on the Sutra label. They certainly made it worth buying the expensive box set.

'Alice In Blunderland' (Alternate version)

An instrumental starting with guitar and marimba duelling, with a guitar solo of wavering notes. It's not so different from the original, but unlike most Beefheart tracks, the playing is lyrical, with a repeating rhythm-guitar refrain and an orthodox lead from Elliot Ingber. The end returns us to a more Beefheartian melody.

'Harry Irene'

The same version from *The Spotlight Kid* Outtakes.

'I Can Not Do This Unless I Can Do This'/'Seam Crooked Sam'

John French is tap-dancing the rhythm, and Don is in full blues mode with harmonica and maracas as he sings the poem over the sparse backing.

'Pompadour Swamp'/'Suction Prints'

This instrumental has nothing to do with the *Bluejeans & Moonbeams* track, but is an early version of the Shiny Beast song 'Suction Prints'. This was culled from a 25-minute jam which provided a number of rhythms that were used later. The track really motors along and was often used to open shows in the early-1970s. The bluesy guitar sets up a fast rhythm before the drums come in with harmonica in the background. There is some blistering lead and extraordinary sounds. At one point, the lead duets with the bass, and there's a burst of marimba at the end.

'The Witch Doctor Life' (Instrumental take)
Drums and bass create a real swampy buzz over the guitar riffs. A second guitar with a different tone, appears, and there's much interweaving as they spar together. The basis of the song was a leftover from the *Mirror Man* sessions. It eventually turned up in a radically different form on Ice Cream For Crow.

'Two Rips In A Haystack'/'Kiss Me My Love'
I have always regarded this to be a rather pedestrian love song, though there is a pleasant marimba part and interesting high-pitched harmonica towards the end.

'Best Batch Yet' (Track, Version 1)
This is disappointing. It sounds like an early play-through of a backing track with a long way to go.

'Your Love Brought Me To Life' (Instrumental)
Another uninspiring track. It's little more than basic groundwork and doesn't stand up well on its own.

'Dirty Blue Gene' (Alternate version 1)
Just the Captain and a dirty guitar. This song has its roots way back in the days of It Comes To You Wrapped In A Brown Paper Bag, and I love this pared-back version. But there was still a way to go before the version that emerged with modified lyrics on Doc At The Radar Station.

'Nowadays A Woman's Gotta Hit A Man' (Early mix)
This thunders along with some great harmonica, like a real blues jam. The horns are prominent and the spiky guitar solo is fabulous. It's Beefheart at his best, creating a different vibe to the *Clear Spot* version.

'Kiss Where I Kain't'
Suddenly we're back in 1967 and *Safe As Milk*, with a driving piece in a relatively simple R&B style. It needs a vocal, though!

'Circumstances' (Alternate version 2)
Don storms in on full throttle with that massive voice of his, then the band blast in, blues harp wailing. For a while, the sound fades with the harp breathing in

and out like a lumbering giant, drums fast but quiet. Then they build up, the band crash back in and we're racing again. Different to *Clear Spot*.

'Little Scratch'

This later emerged on *Clear Spot* as something completely different: 'The Past Sure Is Tense'. The lyrics are quite humorous, the guitar is chirpy, and there's a smattering of harp as bass and guitar mimic each other.

'Dirty Blue Gene' (Alternate version 3)

This version is slightly different, and belts along. It has a great instrumental passage.

This CD is very good, but it still feels like a missed opportunity. There's room for more material, and some of what is there is pedestrian. Having heard the 4-CD bootleg set, I think they could've stuffed a full 70 minutes of excellent material into this package.

Where We Live (A benefit CD for Earthjustice) (2003)

This recording was the last that Don ever made. In 2002, Mike Kappus (Don's booking agent for a number of years) was making a compilation for the environmental group Earthjustice. Many people – including Bob Dylan and Ry Cooder – contributed. Being good friends, Mike wanted Don to contribute something. He suggested that Don change the words of 'Happy Birthday' to become 'Happy Earthday' and sing it to Mother Earth. Don immediately agreed. Despite his disability, he managed to sing the words down the telephone. Given Don's long-standing commitment to environmentalism, it's fitting that his last recording should be such a moving homage to our planet and even more appropriate that he finishes with laughter.

The Live Albums

Sadly, almost all live Captain Beefheart albums are semi-official bootlegs. Labels in certain countries have released recordings of dubious origin (radio broadcasts, club tapes, etc.). Much is of poor quality and only of interest to hardened Beefheart fans.

Most of this material is slung together from bootlegs. Having said that, these are available to us, and a few of them are brilliant historical gems or superb-quality live performances.

The Official Releases
I'm Gonna Do What I Wanna Do (2000)
Personnel:
Don Van Vliet 'Captain Beefheart': vocals, harp, tenor sax, whistling
Jeff Moris Tepper: guitar, slide guitar
Richard Redus: guitar, slide guitar, bass (slide bass), accordion
Bruce Lambourne Fowler: trombone, bass, air bass
Eric Drew Feldman: bass, synthesizer, keyboards
Robert Arthur Williams: drums, percussion
Mary Jane Eisenberg: shaker
Recorded in 1978 at My Father's Place, Roslyn, New York
Producer: Michael Tapes
Engineer: Jeff Kracke
Ben J Adams: photography
Label: Rhino Handmade

If you can't have Zoot Horn Rollo, Rockette Morton, Drumbo, Alex St. Clair or Antennae Jimmy Semens, this is the next best thing and is certainly a huge improvement on the Tragic Band, but I miss the jagged edges of the Trout Mask band. The Captain is certainly on form, and the trombone adds something extraordinary.

My Father's Place is a small venue of around 200 capacity. The audience were at tables eating and listening: an intimate venue for a live recording. The band was on a promo tour for *Shiny Beast (Bat Chain Puller)*. The musicians were hot and well-rehearsed. The material is mostly from that album but with a smattering of other numbers. The quality is excellent. The title comes from the words Don used to berate hecklers.

Tracklist. Disc 1:'Tropical Hot Dog Night', 'Nowadays A Woman's Gotta Hit A Man', 'Owed T' Alex', 'Dropout Boogie', 'Harry Irene', 'Abba Zaba', 'Her Eyes Are A Blue Million Miles', 'Old Fart At Play', 'Well', 'Ice Rose', 'Moonlight On Vermont', 'The Floppy Boot Stomp', 'You Know You're A Man', 'Bat Chain Puller', 'Apes-Ma', 'When I See Mommy I Feel Like A Mummy', 'Veteran's Day Poppy'

Disc 2: Safe As Milk, Suction Prints.

London 1974 (2006)

Personnel:
Don Van Vliet 'Captain Beefheart': vocals, harp
Michael Smotherman: keyboards
Dean Smith: guitar
Paul Uhrig: bass
Ty Grimes: drums
Fuzzy Fuscaldo: guitar
Del Simmons: sax, clarinet, flute
Recorded 9 June 1974 at Theatre Royal, Drury Lane
Producer: Andy DiMartino
Engineers: Alan Perkins, Phill Newell
Label: Virgin

This was the Tragic Band in action: Andy Dimartino's monkeys. I took friends to see this band and was most embarrassed. What a great shame that one of the few Captain Beefheart concerts to be officially recorded had to be with these guys! What I would give for a properly produced live album from the Zoot Horn Rollo era!!

The official Virgin release is worse than the 1993 Movie Gold bootleg version. It has two extra tracks: one of which is the atrocious 'Georgia Brown'.

Tracklist: 'Mirror Man', 'Upon The Me Oh My', 'Full Moon Hot Sun', 'Sugar Bowl', 'Crazy Little Thing', 'This Is The Day', 'New Electric Ride', 'Abba Zabba', 'Peaches', 'Georgia Brown', 'Keep On Rubbing/Mighty Crazy'

The Semi-Official Live Releases

These live albums were put out as radio broadcasts. Copyright resides with the radio stations in many countries, so this music was able to be legally released. The Gonzo and Viper labels specialise in the release of these live broadcasts, many of which have already been circulating as bootlegs for years.

Don's Birthday Party (1994)

Label: Tuff Bites
Recorded live at Showbox, Seattle, 15 January 1981
This concert marked the occasion of Don's 40th birthday. This excellent-quality CD has a relaxed Captain Beefheart and a band on fire and galloping through the numbers. It's wild. The audience sing 'Happy Birthday' in a touching manner. Don berates the audience about the 'smoke smell' (probably cannabis) and complains that he doesn't like 'urine-coloured lights'.

Somewhere Over Vancouver (2009)

Personnel:
Captain Beefheart: vocals, saxophone, Chinese gong
Roy Estrada: bass

Ed Marimba: drums, percussion
Rockette Morton: bass, guitar
Zoot Horn Rollo: slide guitar
Alex St Clair: guitar
Recorded at the Commodore Ballroom, 3 March 1973
Label: Gonzo Multimedia
The band was absolutely red hot at this stage; probably the best ever. But unfortunately, this recording is from an audience bootleg. It's good quality for a bootleg but does no justice to the performance.

An Ashtray Heart (2011)
Toronto Broadcast 17 January 1981
Recorded at the Commodore Ballroom, Vancouver
Label: Leftfield Media
This was actually recorded in Vancouver, not Toronto. The sound quality and balance are great. The 1981 version of the Magic Band is hot. A great show. Unfortunately, the bonus tracks are a disappointment, although the three 1971 tracks had a terrific lineup. The version of 'Orange Claw Hammer' with Frank Zappa, is interesting, and the two 1980 TV tracks are brilliant, though the recording quality is very poor. Such a shame.

The Lost Broadcasts (DVD) (2012)
Label: Gonzo
This features amazing footage of the band in 1972, live in the Radio Bremen TV studio for the German programme *Beat Club*. Great versions of 'Bass Solo', Click Clack', 'Golden Birdies', 'I'm Gonna Booglarize You, Baby' and 'Steal Softly Thru Snow'. The contents of this DVD were later released on vinyl.

Amsterdam '80 (2012)
Personnel:
Captain Beefheart: vocals, harmonica, sax, gongs
Jeff 'Moris' Tepper, Richard 'Midnight Hatsize' Snyder: slide guitar, guitar
Eric Drew Feldman: bass, keyboards
Robert Arthur Williams: drums, percussion
Recorded on 1 November 1980 at the Paradiso, Amsterdam
Label: MLP
A superb concert from the original master tape.

Live 1966-67 (2014)
Label: Keyhole
The first half of this CD is the complete 1966 Avalon Ballroom show that went out on KSAN radio. Five of the tracks were released on the Grow Fins box set, but there are four extra tracks, all with great sound quality. This is Beefheart and his Magic Band as a blues band, covering numbers by Howlin' Wolf, Sonny Boy

Williamson and John Lee Hooker. The cover has mistakes in the information about the second half. These are great early demos from prior to *Safe As Milk*, along with studio performances for John Peel's Top Gear radio show.

Live From Harpos – Somewhere Over Detroit (2014)
Label: Gonzo Multimedia
Live 12/11/1980 at Harpos Concert Theatre, Detroit
This is nothing more than an audience-recorded bootleg and has been circulating for years. Annoying crowd noises intrude at times.

Somewhere Over Paris (2014)
Personnel:
Captain Beefheart: vocals, sax, Chinese gong
Robert Arthur Williams: drums, percussion
Denny Walley, Jeff Moris Tepper: slide guitar
Harry Duncan: harmonica
Eric Drew Feldman: keyboards, synthesizer, bass
Recorded at Paris Hippodrome in 1977
Label: Gonzo Multimedia
This terrible bootleg sounds muffled as if it was recorded underwater. It's a shame because the band was on form and the concert – organised by the French Trotskyist party – was brilliant.

Providence College, Rhode Island 1975 (2015)
Personnel:
Captain Beefheart: vocals, harmonica, sax
Frank Zappa: vocals, guitar
Denny Walley: guitar
Tom Fowler: bass
Terry Bozzio: drums
George Duke: keyboards, vocals
Napoleon Murphy Brock: tenor sax, vocals
Bruce Fowler: trombone
Recorded live at Providence College, Rhode Island on 26 April 1975
Label: Keyhole
Originally recorded by an experienced taper. It's a good-quality show from the Bongo Fury tour, with Don handling the vocals on five tracks. It was first bootlegged as *Muffin Man Goes To College*.

Full Moon In Cowtown (2015)
Label: Iconography
Live from the Cowtown Ballroom, Kansas City on 22 April 1974
This is a good recording of the harmless music of the Tragic Band. It was released as *Live In Kansas City 1974* on the Broadcasting Radio Records label,

and as *Full Moon – Hot Sun Live in Kansas* on the Keyhole label. Previous bootleg releases of this same concert go under the names of *Crazy Little Things* and *Captain Hook*.

Transmission Impossible (2015)
Label: Eat To The Beat
A three-disc set based largely around three already available radio broadcasts, augmented with a few odds and sods, all of which are also widely available.

Disc 1: Tracks 1-9 Radio broadcast from The Avalon Ballroom, San Francisco, 17 June 1967. Tracks 10-18 Various Radio Sessions 1967 and 1968

Disc 2: Live Radio Broadcast from the Cowtown Ballroom, Kansas City, 22 April 1974

Disc 3: Tracks 1-12 Radio broadcast from The Commodore Ballroom, Vancouver, Canada, 17 January 1981. Tracks 13-15 from Tubeworks WABX TV, Detroit 15 January 1971. Track 16 from a KWST FM Radio Show broadcast with Frank Zappa, 1 November 1975. Tracks 17-18 from Saturday Night Live, November 1980

Somewhere Over California (2016)
Personnel:
Captain Beefheart: vocals, harp, sax, gong
Denny Walley: slide guitar
Jeff Moris Tepper, Richard Snyder: guitar
Eric Drew Feldman: bass, keyboards
Robert Arthur Williams: drums, percussion
Recorded on 29 January 1981, Live At The Country Club, Reseda, California
Label: Gonzo Multimedia
A release of a widely circulated bootleg called *Best Batch Yet*. The band was on fire, and this has good sound quality for a gig recorded in this way.

The Broadcast Archives (4 CDs) (2019)
Label: The Broadcast Archive
Nothing more than a repackaging of three bootleg in a cardboard case:
Full Moon in Cowtown: Live 1974 Radio Broadcast
Plastic Factory: Avalon Ballroom, San Francisco 1966 (plus bonus tracks)
The Muffin Man Goes to College: Rhode Island 1975, Bongo Fury Tour

Live In Vancouver 1981 (2019)
Personnel:
Captain Beefheart: vocals, harmonica, sax, gong
Jeff Moris Tepper, Richard Snyder: slide guitar, guitar

Denny Walley: slide guitar
Eric Drew Feldman: bass, keyboards
Robert Arthur Williams: drums, percussion
Broadcast live by CBC at the Commodore Ballroom, Vancouver, on 17 January 1981
Label: Keyhole
An excellent concert with very good sound quality.

The Bootleg Albums

Although these are available to purchase from many legal sources, their providence is extremely suspect. Some boots are good quality but others are of inferior quality. Information is often wrong; packaging poor and the sound quality is often atrocious.

What's All This Booga Booga Music? (1975)

A bootleg from the Troubadour in Los Angeles in 1973 – of particular interest because it contains the only known recording of the song 'Jimmy Bill's In Town'. It also features the blues numbers 'Black Snake Blues' and 'I'm A King Bee'.

Live At The Radar Station (1994)

A Bloodshot Rollin' Red Production. A classic Beefheart bootleg that first appeared on vinyl and later became a double CD.

Out Here Over There (1998)

This is a particularly important bootleg, because, although the sound quality is only good, it compiles all the John Peel Top Gear recordings, including the rare version of 'Electricity' and the seven-minute 'Trust Us'.

Russian Flexi Discs (Late 1990s)

These are worth a mention because they're so weird! They are 6" square, single-sided, brightly coloured flexi discs consisting of just one song (longer songs were shortened to fit). A large number of them were produced in small numbers each but remain undocumented.

Mersey Trout (2000)

Label: MilkSafe productions/Ozit Morpheus
Recorded at Rotters Club, Liverpool, 29 October 1980
Unusually this one has great sound quality, and the band is blistering!!

Dust Sucker (2002)

Label: Ozit Morpeus
A bootleg release of the original *Bat Chain Puller* album tapes from Paramount Studios as touted to Virgin records by Roger Eagles. Unlike the

official Zappa Family Trust release, these tracks have not been remastered, and consequently stand up poorly against the official release. The title Dust Sucker relates to Don's short job as a vacuum cleaner salesman. The seven bonus tracks are six poor quality live recordings and a studio recording of 'Well Well Well' featuring Mark 'Rockette Morton' Boston on vocals.

Magnetic Hands – Live In The UK – 1972-1980 (2002)
Label: Viper

A live album put together from performances throughout the UK. Unfortunately, some tracks are poor quality and many have come from bootleg sources. It's interesting to hear the range of material, and also for blues standards like 'Old Black Snake' and 'Sugar Mama' to get an outing.

Railroadism – Live In The USA 1972-1981 (2003)
Label: Viper

Another live recording, taken from the USA tours. The sound quality on this CD is much better – good-to-excellent throughout – and it's packed with rarities and tremendous performances. As it's a companion to Magnetic Hands, they tried to use different songs, so there is only a little overlap between the two.

We are treated to a couple of the old blues tracks 'Old Black Snake' and 'King Bee'. Other outstanding tracks include 'The Blimp' (sung by Harry Duncan), an incredibly rare version of 'Railroadism' (a close cousin of the fabulous 'Hoboism'), a strange 'I'm Gonna Booglarize You, Baby', a powerful 'The Dust Blows Forward 'N The Dust Blows Back', and some fabulous whistling on 'Harry Irene'. There are blistering versions of 'Smithsonian Institute Blues' and 'Big Eyed Beans from Venus', and the set concludes with 'Avalon Blues' from the 1966 Avalon Ballroom concert.

It's an excellent live album showing just how powerful and brilliant Don and His Magic Bands were in concert.

Dichotomy (2004)
Label: Ozit Morpheus

Once again, Ozit has compiled a shoddy mess of rarities, outtakes and demos, seized semi-legally from a variety of sources. There seems no logic to the sequencing or selection. There are no details, and they've even taken the liberty of altering some track titles! Blasphemy!!

The lengthy Spotlight Kid Outtakes blues jams between Don and Zoot Horn Rollo or Winged Eel Fingerling, have been edited to produce 'Key To The Highway', 'Scratch My Back' and 'Sun Zoom Spark'. There are a number of short spoken-word sections lifted from various interviews: 'This is Captain Beefheart', 'Comment', 'Winnebago Sioux' and 'Skeleton Key'. Rather irritatingly, there are few worthy tracks amongst this mishmash of songs ranging from 1966 to the late-1970s.

Prime Quality Beef (2005)

Label: Ozit Morpheus

Another poor-quality bootleg and a bewildering combination of live and studio songs. It's mostly songs from the 1974 Kansas City Cowtown concert (the sequence jumbled up for no apparent reason), with the duplication of 'Peaches'. These live recordings are interspersed with a few of the unprocessed tracks from *Mirror Man*. It makes no sense to me and is hardly what I would describe as prime-quality beef – it's more a low-quality burger from Sid's Greasy Spoon.

Poet Rock Musicians Of The Desert – Rare Phrases And Poems From Captain Beefheart and his Magic Band and Jim Morrison (of The Doors) (2007)

Label: Ozit Morpheus

A bunch of poems plucked from a variety of sources, with the bogus lame excuse of both Don and Jim Morrison being 'Desert Poets'. The reality is that they have very little in common.

For some reason, there are two versions of Gary Lucas reciting 'One Man Sentence'.

Nan True's Hole Vols 1, 2 & 3 (2011/2012)

Label: Ozit Morpheus/Dandelion

These are poor quality recordings from 1972/1973, supposedly from John Peel's own collection. The nearest they probably were to John Peel is that he may have been in the audience. Peel Acres (John Peel's country house) was originally called Nan True's Hole. Unfortunately, the recordings are not Peel's: they've been gleaned from various bootlegs.

Son Of Dust Sucker (2012)

Label: Ozit Morpheus/Dandelion

This is a re-release of the same *Bat Chain Puller* material as the original *Dust Sucker*, though not upgraded or remastered. There is a different set of mystery bonus tracks to the ones on the original *Dust Sucker*. These are nine low-quality live bootleg recordings from Paris in 1972 and Detroit in 1971.

Vol 1 – Translucent Fresnel (Live 1972/1973)

A Fresnel is a lens in a spotlight: an allusion to *The Spotlight Kid*, which is the album the tour was promoting. The concert is largely from Leicester University 1973, with two tracks from Manchester. The quality is poor, which is a shame because the performances were superb.

Vol 2 – The Nan True's Hole Tapes – Live Spring 1972

An improvement in quality from Vol 1. and probably sourced from the Royal Albert Hall 1972 concert.

Vol 3 – The Nan True's Hole Tapes – Live in the UK
An extremely poor bootleg of what is largely the 1975 Knebworth concert.

Easy Teeth (2015)
Label: Gonzo Multimedia
A poor-quality recording of the great concert on 18 February 1978 at The Golden Bear, Huntington Beach, CA.

CB & MB In GB (2015)
Label: Ozit Morpheus
These are bootleg recordings from around the UK between 1972 and 1980. As one might expect, the sound quality is variable given the sources. They include audience recordings from Knebworth 1975 and Manchester 1980. The spoken-word on disc 2 consists of snippets from Don, Ry Cooder and Frank Zappa, with a longer eight-minute interview with the Liverpool DJ and promoter Roger Eagle.

Captain's Last Live Concert Plus... (2015)
Label: Ozit Morpheus
Recorded on 31 January 1981 at the Golden Bear, CA.
This was an historic event, as it was the Captain's last-ever show. The band is excellent and the recording is good quality, although it has annoying hiss. The bonus tracks feature the widely available radio version of 'Orange Claw Hammer' with Frank Zappa, snippets from a John Peel interview and a section from a BBC documentary with Ry Cooder talking about *Safe As Milk*.

Live At Bickershaw Festival (2015)
Personnel: Captain Beefheart: vocals, sax, harmonica, Zoot Horn Rollo: slide guitar, guitar, Winged Eel Fingerling: slide guitar, bass, Rockette Morton: bass, guitar, Orejon: bass, Ed Marimba: drums, percussion, Recorded live in 1972, Label: Ozit Morpheus
A superb set played at 4 a.m.!! The recording is from an audience tape made by a fanzine editor. It's a good recording given the recording equipment used.

Live at Knebworth 1975 (2016)
Label: Ozit Morpheus/Dandelion
Recorded from a fan bootleg with a quality that's only fair-to-good.
Frank Zappa And Captain Beefheart (2019)
Label: Studio Hamburg
Recycled material from a variety of Zappa shows, assembled for digital distribution only.

Mallard

Following the 1974 recording of *Unconditionally Guaranteed*, the Magic Band was in despair. They believed in the wonders of *Trout Mask* and *Decals*, and held the Captain in awe. However, they'd reached the end of their tether. For years they'd been starved, bullied, mentally intimidated and occasionally physically abused. They'd received little money and had been living on food stamps and hand-outs from relatives and friends. They had survived on hope, promises and the knowledge that they were producing music that was unique, superb and different, and that stretched them to their limits. Then things changed.

While *The Spotlight Kid* and *Clear Spot* were brilliant bluesy albums, the band had found the simpler style boring. It wasn't stretching them the same. Nor had the change to a more commercial sound brought success and riches. The band might have been regarded in music circles as geniuses, but that wasn't paying any bills. They were also getting older. They weren't the malleable young kids they'd been half a decade before and were now more prepared to stand up for themselves. They had not liked the way the DiMartino brothers had muscled in and were calling the shots. When the band heard the final tapes for *Unconditionally Guaranteed*, it proved to be the final straw. They were appalled. They felt that not only was the music simple, but the mix and overdubs had completely obscured any of their decent playing. They hated it. Following a band discussion, they concluded that they'd reached the end, and four of them walked out: Alex Snouffer, Bill Harkleroad, Mark Boston and Artie Tripp. This caused great acrimony. Don's contracted tours of Europe and the USA were only a few weeks away, and suddenly he had no band.

The band was also in confusion. They'd moved back to Northern California, and in order to earn some money fast, they set about playing some local gigs. This is when things started to become difficult. They discovered they were unable to use the name The Magic Band. Nor were they allowed to use the stage names Don had given them. These were all part of the contract they'd signed with Don's management God's Golfball. Alex soon left. John French, John Thomas and Mark Marcellino (ex-Magic Banders) joined up with the remaining three, and set about rehearsing and playing low-key gigs. John French was actually doing vocals, and Art was drumming. Unfortunately, that early band broke up before it got going. John French parted ways with the others, ironically to link up with Don again. The band still used some of the compositions they had worked on with him.

Instead of continuing in the Magic Band style as one might imagine they would – after all, one of the main reasons they'd become so disaffected was the move away from the challenging music – they set about creating a different sound. To that end, they introduced Sam Galpin on vocals and piano. Sam was an unlikely choice in that he was a country-tinged bar singer who'd never heard of the Magic Band.

This is where Jethro Tull's Ian Anderson comes into the picture. He was a big Magic Band fan and a good friend of Mark Boston, and used his influence to secure them a deal with Virgin Records in the UK. Ian also offered them the use of his portable studio, a country house to stay in, and he financed the project. It was all too good to be true. Apprehensively, they set off to England, where John 'Rabbit' Bundrick (of Free fame) came in on Fender Rhodes electric piano for the recording.

The name Mallard came about because they had to give out a press release, and at the time they'd been working on a song called 'Mallard Ballad'.

Don disdainfully called them a bunch of quacks. They produced two albums without great success, before finally calling it a day.

Mallard (1975)
Personnel:
Bill Harkleroad: acoustic and electric guitars
Mark Boston: bass (vocals on 'Winged Tuskadero')
Art Tripp III: drums, percussion, marimba
Sam Galpin: vocals (piano on 'Desperadoes')
John 'Rabbit' Bundrick: Fender Rhodes piano ('One Day Once', 'A Piece Of Me', 'Reign Of Pain')
Barry Morgan: Latin percussion ('Reign Of Pain')
Recorded at Ian Anderson's portable studio, Devonshire; Maison Rouge mobile
Producer: Bill Harkleroad
Producer, engineer: Robin Black
Label: Virgin

It feels as if the band was deliberately avoiding the Captain Beefheart style, and trying for a sound of their own. Sam Galpin's deep voice has a totally different quality, and there was a move away from the jagged, spiky notes, weaving guitars, polyrhythms and dissonance. This album is much more mainstream and orthodox. It worked well, but didn't push any boundaries. It was quite country-tinged: maybe that was just the element Sam brought with him. If anyone was expecting a reprise of the Magic Band, they were in for a disappointment. Mallard were very good, but they weren't trying to be the Magic Band.

'Back On The Pavement' (Wagstaff, Harkleroad)
A great number with acoustic guitars, slide, and Sam's deep voice. A Vietnam vet is back on the pavement doing everything a working man can do.

'She's Long And She's Lean' (Alvy, Harkleroad, Boston,)
A Beefheart-ish track with some great guitar. A different vibe though.

'Road To Morrocco' (Harkleroad, Boston)
This was much more lyrical than Beefheart ever was; an instrumental that gallops along.

'One Day Once' (French, Harkleroad)
Gentle, with interesting slide guitar and an acoustic vibe.

'Yellow' (Harkleroad)
An acoustic guitar piece with some fine fretwork. Melodic.

'Desperadoes Waiting For A Train' (Clark) (Arr. Jim Dickenson)
More country. A tale from the wild west.

'A Piece Of Me' (French, Harkleroad)
Some excellent elements in a standard format. That last slide note sounds like Zoot's lunar note.

'Reign Of Pain' (Moore, French, Harkleroad)
Nice synchronised guitar-playing. Sam possesses a good singing voice.

'South Of The Valley' (French) (Arr. Harkleroad)
A laid-back Eagles feel.

'Winged Tuskadero' (Wagstaff, Harkleroad)
A track with more punch and innovation.

'Peon' (Donald Van Vliet (sic))
This is the one Beefheart song on the album, but it's done completely differently, as if to emphasise the change. The brutality of the playing has been replaced by delicate flowing beauty. Complete with bird-singing, it's been transformed.

In A Different Climate (1976)
Personnel:
Bill Harkleroad: guitars
John Thomas: keyboards, backing vocals
Sam Galpin: vocals
Mark Boston: bass, Dobro (vocals 'Old Man Grey')
George Draggota: drums
John McFee: pedal steel guitar ('Harvest')
Recorded at Clearwell Castle, Monmouth on the Manor Mobile
Producer/Engineer: Robert John 'Mutt' Lange
Engineer: Michel Glossop
Label: Virgin Records (UK), CBS (USA)

The second album is even more country in style than the first and is not as captivating. It's enjoyable enough but presents nothing groundbreaking. Too easy listening and mainstream for me.

'Green Coyote' (Wagstaff, Harkleroad, Boston)

The album starts with an up-tempo country feel. The guitar is sweet. We're in for more of the same.

'Your Face On Someone Else' (Wagstaff, Harkleroad, Thomas)

A slow song about love lost.

'Harvest' (Wagstaff, Thomas)

Another country song, complete with steel guitar and backing singers, on the theme of a life spent on whisky and women, with eventual salvation.

'Mama Squeeze' (Harkleroad)

A standard arrangement for an unexceptional song.

'Heartstrings' (Harkleroad, Thomas)

This has nice bass, and Zoot plays nice guitar. But who ever thought I'd be talking about Zoot and 'nice' in the same sentence? A jazz feel gets going towards the end.

'Old Man Grey' (Boston)

More experimental backing, but spoiled by Sam's saccharine country recitation. It's a million miles away from Beefheart.

'Texas Weather' (Alvy, Harkleroad)

'Old Man Grey' segues into 'Texas Weather': another country song.

'Big Foot' (Alvy, Harkleroad)

This ain't no monster. It's good enough, but nothing exceptional. Like the rest of the album, it doesn't set you on fire.

The Magic Band – Reformed

It was 2003, and it was with trepidation that I ventured to the Irish Centre in Leeds for my first gig seeing the newly reformed Magic Band. What was a Magic Band without Beefheart going to be like? I was expecting only a weak, insipid tribute act, but they blew me away with a full-throttle Beefheart performance.

John French was the instigator. Matt Groening – creator of *The Simpsons*, and a huge Beefheart fan – had asked French to form a band for the 2003 All Tomorrows Parties festival. Don grudgingly gave his blessing. They were free to the band name and the stage names. The lineup was John 'Drumbo' French on drums, lead vocals and harmonica, Gary 'Mantis' Lucas and Denny 'Feelers Rebo' Walley on guitars, Mark 'Rockette Morton' Boston on bass, and Robert Williams on drums for the vocal numbers. Robert Williams was replaced by Michael Traylor for the European tour that followed. They played a lot of gigs, and I was able to get to a number of them. The excitement was there and the band was so tight. Though nobody could come near to matching Don, John French was superb on the vocals. I hardly missed the Captain!! French made quite a frontman. He looked the part and was far more animated than the Captain ever was. Nobody could emulate the Captain's vocal range and tonality, but John was no slouch.

Their aim was to keep the music of Captain Beefheart alive and remain faithful to his compositions. As John had been music arranger for much of the Captain's material, this wasn't too difficult a task. He knew the songs inside out. Those live performances had the same energy as the Captain's original bands, and it was like rediscovering a loved one after a separation of decades. Ecstasy.

Following that tour, the band sadly broke up, but they were back in 2011 with a slightly different lineup. Eric Klerks replaced Gary Lucas, and Craig Bunch replaced Michael Traylor. The changes didn't detract from the band's brilliance. They went on to tour every year and survived further lineup changes. Denny Walley left to be replaced by Max Kutner, and they brought in a keyboard player: first Brian Havey and then Jonathan Sindleman. Rockette Morton was unable to play on their farewell tour because he had a triple bypass. Jonathan played the bass parts on keyboards. By this time, the band was not quite as good, but they still produced a fabulous show.

The last gig I saw was again at the Irish Centre in Leeds: sadly a rather grouchy affair. The band was beset with sound problems, and John became very annoyed. Despite all that, I enjoyed the gig, but it was a sad way to go out. They weren't at their best.

That was it. It was not enough. They'd given me ten bonus years of quality Beef. I'd seen them at numerous gigs all over the country and revelled in this unexpected gift. What I cherish most was a chance to sit down with the band after a show and chew the fat. I cleared up a number of queries, shared some memories, and relived those fabulous Beefheart years of the 1960s and 1970s.

Coincidentally, versions of Love, Country Joe and the Fish, Quicksilver Messenger Service, Big Brother and The Holding Company and even The

Doors reformed and were touring. I caught Further (the ashes of Grateful Dead) in San Francisco. For a short time it felt like the 1960s all over again. But the Magic Band was the best!! I have hundreds of photos, great memories and some outstanding albums.

Back To The Front (2003)

Personnel:
John 'Drumbo' French: vocals, drums, harmonica
Mark 'Rockette Morton' Boston: bass
Gary 'Mantis' Lucas, Denny 'Feelers Rebo' Walley: guitar
Studio: Paradoxx Sound, Palmdale, CA
Producers: Bob Weston, John 'Drumbo' French
Tim Sutton, Gary Lucas: photography
Matt Groening: liner notes
Label: ATP Recordings

This mixture of instrumental interpretations and vocal tracks was recorded virtually live in the studio. It has many Beefheart hallmarks: incredible drumming, weaving guitars, pounding bass. The songs are all Beefheart classics, ranging from *Safe As Milk* through to *Clear Spot*. The vocals – which could've been the weak link – sound great. Even if using the same band, re-recordings rarely recapture the vitality of the originals, but these do.

The band set out to keep the music of the Captain alive, and they certainly did that. They worked through a selection of classic Beefheart tracks and did justice to them all. This was no tribute band: this was the real thing.

Matt Groening – who was instrumental in bringing them back together – wrote the liner notes, and you can tell he was every bit as impressed as I was.

21st Century Mirror Men (2004)

Personnel:
John 'Drumbo' French: vocals, drums, harmonica
Mark 'Rockette Morton' Boston: bass
Gary 'Mantis' Lucas, Denny 'Feelers Rebo' Walley: guitar
Robert Arthur Williams, Michael Traylor: drums on vocal songs
Recorded live at the Royal Festival Hall; Liquid Room, Edinburgh; Rescue Rooms, Nottingham; The Garage, London; All Tomorrow's Parties festival in Los Angeles
Producer: John 'Drumbo' French
Engineer: Bob Weston (Live recording)
Chris Musto: artwork, photography
Ralf Nygard: film editor, cameraman
Label: Proper Records

A live album put together by John 'Drumbo' French. He sorted through seven complete concerts to select the best performances. I was fortunate to catch them at The Rescue Rooms in Nottingham, and I can confirm they were hot. We had an exciting evening. These tracks confirm that.

There is a little overlap with the material on Back To The Front, but the dynamic of playing in front of an audience creates something special. The recording quality is superb. The package comes with a DVD featuring seven tracks recorded at Camber Sands, but I can't say it's the best recording.

The Magic Band – Oxford, UK, 6 June 2005
Personnel:
John 'Drumbo' French: vocals, drums, harmonica
Mark 'Rockette Morton' Boston: bass
Gary 'Mantis' Lucas, Denny 'Feelers Rebo' Walley: guitar
Michael Traylor: drums on vocal songs
Recorded live at The Zodiac (Carling Academy) Oxford, UK
Producer: John 'Drumbo' French
Label: Sundazed

This superbly recorded live gig of the first reunited incarnation of the Magic Band produced a brilliant fun reminder of just how good they were.

The Magic Band Plays The Music Of Captain Beefheart – Live London 2013
Personnel:
John 'Drumbo' French: vocals, drums, harmonica
Mark 'Rockette Morton' Boston: bass
Denny 'Feelers Rebo' Walley, Eric Klerks: guitar
Craig Bunch: drums (except on 'Alice In Blunderland')
Recorded live at 'Under The Bridge, Chelsea
Producer: John 'Drumbo' French
Engineers: Paul Riley, Barry 'Bazz' Farmer
Label: Proper Records

A recording of the last gig of the 2013 tour, which marked the tenth anniversary of their reunion. The band fed off the energy of a capacity audience to produce a blistering show. Fabulous. A DVD called *Singing Through You* was made of the concert, which had four extra tracks from the show. This time the filming was professional, with excellent sound quality and editing. It was produced by Elaine Shepherd – who previously made the documentary The Artist Formerly Known As Captain Beefheart – and incorporated material shot by the audience.

And that was it. We had a brilliant extra ten years of superb Beefheart music – not quite the real thing, but near enough. It was all over.

So John, if you are reading this, it would be wonderful if you could gather some of the surviving alumni for one last hurrah. Zoot, Mantis, Rockette, Eric, Feelers Rebo, Moris, Antennae, Robert – another final gathering would be sublime.

The Alumni and their solo music

Various members of the Magic Band – and there have been many over the years – have progressed to solo careers and produced a number of superb albums. I feel this is worthy of mention because anyone who was exposed to the Captain and his perspective of music, was bound to be influenced by it. I don't propose to review the following albums, but if you wish to continue on this journey, this list will show you where to look.

John 'Drumbo' French
1987 Crazy Backwards Alphabet
1987 Live, Love, Larf & Loaf
1990 Invisible Means
1994 Waiting on the Flame
1998 O Solo Drumbo
2007 Crazy Backwards Alphabet II
2008 City of Refuge

Bill 'Zoot Horn Rollo' Harkleroad
2001 We Saw a Bozo Under the Sea
2014 Masks

Mark 'Rockette Morton' Boston
2003 Love Space

Jeff 'Antennae Jimmy Semens' Cotton
1971 MU
1974 The Last Album (Released 1981)
1974 Children Of The Rainbow (Released 1985)
2022 The Fantasy of Reality

Elliot 'Winged Eel Fingerling' Ingber
2001 The The The The 4

Denny 'Feelers Rebo' Walley
1997 Spare Parts

Robert Williams
1981 Buy My Record
1982 Late One Night
1998 Date With The Devil's Daughter
2016 Temporarily Immortal (As Beefheart Jr.)

Jeff 'Moris' Tepper
1996 Big Enough to Disappear

1998 Sundowner, Eggtooth
2000 Moth to Mouth
2004 Head Off
2008 Stingray in the Heart
2010 A Singer Named Shotgun Throat

Moris has also worked with PJ Harvey, Tom Waits, Gary Lucas, 17 Pygmies and Frank Black.

Gary 'Mantis' Lucas
1991 Skeleton at the Feast
1992 Gods and Monsters
1994 Bad Boys of the Arctic
1996 Pražská Strašidla (The Ghosts of Prague) (with Urfaust)
1997 Evangeline
1998 Busy Being Born
1999 @ Paradiso
2000 The Du-Tels – No Knowledge of Music Required (with Peter Stampfel)
2000 Street of Lost Brothers
2000 Level the Playing Field: Early Hurly Burly 1988-1994
2001 The Edge of Heaven
2002 Songs to No One 1991-1992 (with Jeff Buckley)
2003 Operators Are Standing By: The Essential Gary Lucas 1989-1996
2003 Diplopia (with Jozef van Wissem)
2004 The Universe of Absence (with Jozef van Wissem)
2005 Fast 'n' Bulbous – Pork Chop Blue Around the Rind
2006 Coming Clean
2007 Musical Blazeup with DJ Cosmo
2008 The Dark Poets – Beyond the Pale
2008 Chase the Devil (with Dean Bowman)
2008 Rock the Joint (with Beardyman)
2008 Down the Rabbit Hole (with Gerald Zbindin)
2008 Purple Somersault (with DJ Cosmo)
2009 Fast 'n' Bulbous – Waxed Oop
2009 Rishte (with Najma Akhtar)
2010 'Music for the Eden Project'/'Q & A'
2011 The Ordeal of Civility
2012 Gary Lucas Plays Bohemian Classics, Czech Republic
2013 Popular Science (with M'Lumbo)
2013 Cinefantastique
2014 Other World (with Peter Hammill)
2016 Fleischerei
2016 Pearly Clouds
2016 Stereopticon (with Jann Klose)

2017 The World of Captain Beefheart
2019 The Complete Jeff Buckley and Gary Lucas Songbook
2021 The Essential Gary Lucas

Eric Drew Feldman
2004 Knife & Fork – Miserycord

Alex St. Claire
1972 Denny King And The B. O. Boogie Band – Evil Wind Is Blowing

Rick Snyder
1996 The Mystery Band – Insert Title Here
2000 The Mystery Band – Leo Gemini Capricorns & Jones Ltd

Tributes and Covers

The real importance of a band or artist can perhaps be judged by the number of people who are influenced by them or want to cover their work. There are numerous bands – from The Beatles to The White Stripes – who respect Don and his music. The list is endless. But possibly in the music of PJ Harvey, The Fall and Tom Waits is where Don's impact can be most distinctly heard.

Certain covers of Beefheart songs stand out to me:

The Edgar Broughton Band cover of 'Dropout Boogie'/'Apache'. (I used to love bopping about to this at free festivals in the 1960s). They seemed to model themselves on the Captain.

Juicy Lucy did a fabulous version of 'Willie The Pimp'.

The White Stripes produced the tribute single 'Party Of Special Things To Do'/'China Pig'/'Ashtray Heart'.

The Kills covered 'Dropout Boogie' on their 2002 *Black Rooster* EP.

The Fall produced covers of 'Beatle Bones 'N' Smokin' Stones' and 'Drop Out Boogie'.

The Three Johns covered 'Moonlight On Vermont'.

Magazine did 'I Love You, You Big Dummy'.

The Black Keys produced a cover of 'I'm Glad'.

The Meridian Arts Ensemble performed six wonderful interpretations of Don's work on their 1995 *Prime Meridian* album – big band jazz, orchestral versions and some spoken word. The same album also included music by Stravinsky and Zappa.

The Henry Kaiser Band scattered Beefheart covers through their many albums.

Joan Osborne did an excellent cover of '(His) Eyes Are A Blue Million Miles'.

The Cramps did a version of 'Hard Workin' Man'.

The Tubes included a cover of 'My Head Is My Only House Unless It Rains' on their third album *Now*, and even managed to get Don to play saxophone on 'Cathy's Clone'.

Quite a range of covers!

There are also a few tribute compilation albums. Fast 'N' Bulbous (2005) was the first one. That was followed by *Neon Meate Dream Of A Octofish*, which featured some even weirder covers. The best and most inventive arrangements were on the 2005 album *Mama Kangaroos* – a collective of female bands from Philadelphia, and probably the most unlikely source for brilliant Beefheart covers.

There are many bands that specialise in producing albums of Beefheart material. The foremost of these is the wonderful Fast 'N' Bulbous band featuring the great Gary Lucas. Gary was the superb guitarist who played in the Magic Band back in the *Doc at the Radar Station* and *Ice Cream for Crow* days. He went from fan to friend to important band member, and ended up as Don's manager. Gary formed Fast 'N' Bulbous with Phillip Johnston and his band that consisted of sax, trumpet, trombone, bass and drums – an unusual mix of instruments for playing guitar-driven Beefheart classics, yet they did it. Gary played the only guitar, with the horns playing the other guitar parts. They produced two albums: *Pork Chop Blue Around The Rind* (2005) and *Waxed Oop* (2009). The former focussed more on the *Trout Mask Replica* era, while *Waxed Oop* had songs from as far back as *Safe As Milk* and *Strictly Personal*.

Gary went on to produce an intriguing project with Co de Kloet called 'I Have A Cat', in which they put Don's last interview to music. In 2015, Gary staged The World Of Captain Beefheart live in Amsterdam with the Metropole Orchestra and singer Nona Hendryx. He went on to produce a groundbreaking album with her in 2017: *The World Of Captain Beefheart*. It consists of Gary's interpretations of Don's songs using Nona's superb vocals.

Edinburgh's Orange Claw Hammer gave their interpretation of Beefheart with a spirit of adventure and mischief on *Cooks the Beef* in 2016 and *New Beef Dreams* in 2021.

Ben Waters (aka Benjamin Horrendous from the Fourfathers) produced a solo rendering of Beefheart songs called *Messin' with the Kid*, which consists of blues interpretations of songs from *The Spotlight Kid*.

Men And Volts started life as a Beefheart cover band with the fabled *A Giraffe is Listening to the Radio*, before going on to produce their own Beefheart-inspired numbers.

It doesn't end there. It seems that tribute bands are popping up all over the place – Al Lover, The Beefheart Toronto Project, Big Eyed Beans From Venus, Doctor Dark, Lewis Taylor, Men and Volts, 21st Century Men, Robyn Hitchcock and the Imaginary Band, Rosa Ensemble, Old Farts At Play, and Van Goo...

Afterword

It's 40 years since Captain Beefheart ended his musical career and 12 years since his death. Many bands have been influenced by his music and poetry, and his cult status has grown. His musical legacy is awe-inspiring. A stream of fabulous musicians passed through his bands. In my view, they were all magic bands (bar one).

In the course of writing this book, I totally immersed in Captain Beefheart's music. I played every album and studied every track. I listened to the live albums, bootlegs and dubious semi-legal offerings. The experience has been fabulous but daunting. There has been pressure in trying to do justice to an artist I have admired for over 54 years. I had to listen to the tracks with an analytical mind, which has not been easy. I have tried to provide background information, give my honest evaluations and bring the music to life. I hope I have succeeded.

Don Van Vliet is unique. His music deserves to be played, enthused over and remembered. He has made my life richer, and I remain in awe of his creativity.

Thank you!!

Opher Goodwin, 22 February 2022

Bibliography

Barnes, M., *Captain Beefheart* (Music Sales Corporation – 2000)
French, J., *Through the Eyes of Magic* (Proper Music Publishing Ltd -14 Oct. 2013)
Harkleroad, B., James, B., *Lunar Notes – Zoot Horn Rollo's Captain Beefheart experience* (Gonzo Multimedia - 9 Jun. 2013)
Courrier, K., *Trout Mask Replica (*Continuum - 1 Dec. 2008)
Brooks, K., *Captain Beefheart – Tin Teardrop* (Agenda Ltd - 1 Feb. 2000)
Cruickshank, B., *Fast And Bulbous – The Story of Captain Beefheart* (Agenda Ltd - 1 July 1996)
Wade, C., *The Music of Captain Beefheart* – album reviews and Magic Band interviews (Lulu.com; Illustrated edition - 10 Feb. 2015)
Webb, C., *Captain Beefheart – The Man and his Music* (Kawabata Press, 1987)